A HEART
ACCORDING TO GOD

ISBN: 978-2-95-646162-3
© Published by Pascal Malonda, Paris, 2020

Original title: UN CŒUR SELON DIEU
Translation: Othmane Chanaoui

A HEART
ACCORDING TO GOD

PASCAL MALONDA

*By the size of one's heart,
you can measure one's greatness.*

Pascal Malonda

*"People judge by outward appearance,
but the Lord looks at the heart."*

(1 Samuel 16:7)

Introduction

On May 26, 2018, a 4-year-old young boy was hanging over emptiness, dangling to the fourth-floor balcony of a building in Paris. His father, who was away to go shopping, left him unattended. Several passersby were present on the scene, powerless. Among them, Mamoudou Gassama, a 23-year-old Malian young man, showed outstanding bravery and managed to climb the front of the building at the risk of his life with bare hands. He pulled the child to safety back onto the balcony while the people below were cheering and crying with relief. The scene, which was filmed by passersby, has been watched several thousands of times on social networks. His feat was quickly relayed by mainstream media in France and abroad, which resulted in an invitation at the Elysee Palace to meet Emmanuel Macron, the French president. He congratulated and rewarded him with granting him the French citizenship. The naturalization order, published in the Federal Register and signed by Prime Minister Édouard Philippe, points out that: *"This act of great bravery has perfectly exemplified some of the values that contribute to put together the members of the national community such as bravery, disinterest, selflessness, attention paid to the most vulnerable.*[1]*"* The congratulations have not come to an end at that point, since Mamoudou Gassama has been hosted to

---

1. Official journal of September 12, 2018/ N°210: (https//: www.legifrance.gouv.fr)

the Paris city hall to get the Medal of the City of Paris, and to the United States for the "BET Humanitarian Award" prize, attributed by the TV channel BET[2], which rewards people who have shown bravery during the year. He has also been invited to Mali to meet the Malian president Ibrahim Boubacar Keïta, not forgetting the Paris Fire Department squad that has offered him to join them. His heroic act has thoroughly changed his life and enabled him to gain access to some people he should never have met otherwise.

There are so to speak two kinds of heroes: the classic hero and the hero according to God. Both stand up for values, even a cause they deem good; however, the big difference is that a hero according to God is someone according to the heart of God, who tries at all costs to do His will. The classic hero gets admired by people for what he has done or for what he is, even if some heroes obtain recognition only long after they pass away. The hero according to God will win top honors in his moment as well, but this time from God Himself. At the end of his journey, Jesus Christ will welcome him with these words: *"Come and share your master's happiness, my good and faithful servant"* (Matthew 25:23). By crossing the doorstep, he will be amazed to hear the ovation from the people he would have driven to Christ, as well as from angels. Everyone who has the life of Jesus Christ as a model will be greeted as a hero, because He Himself is the ultimate Hero. The election criteria being quite different from those we may generally know, nobody can foresee the rewards he will inherit, because what truly animates our heart will determine the worth of every action we have made. That is why the Bible warns us not to judge the others too early, because only God, who tests the hearts, genuinely knows us, as it is shown in this verse:

____

2. BET: Black Entertainment Television

> *"Therefore judge nothing before the appointed time; wait until the Lord comes. He will bring to light what is hidden in darkness and will expose the motives of the heart. At that time each will receive their praise from God."*
> (1 Corinthians 4:5)

If society likes to consider people according to what they have done, the same is totally different in the Kingdom of God, since by **the size of one's heart, you can measure one's greatness**. One day, every heart will be unveiled before God and everyone will stand facing the mirror of his soul. By seeing the seasons and events that have punctuated our existence passing before our eyes, a strong belief will then be marked in us. We will know very clearly, at this very moment, if we were someone according to the heart of God or not. The light of his revelation will come and enlighten our mind and remove the intellectual, cultural, environmental and societal veil which prevented us from seeing Him as He really is. The non-believers will no longer have any doubt whatsoever about the existence of God, but unfortunately, it will be too late. In the same way, a separation will be made between those who claim to be believers and true believers.

How to be someone according to the heart of God? How to have a heart in which God holds a central place, a heart full of love, honest, true, humble, not judging others, loving everybody in the same way, serving his neighbor, obedient and making God's will? Here is the whole subject of this book. These characteristics particularly concern the heart of God, but the people who show this kind of attitude are often put aside, because the world is more and more individualistic and dominated by a competitive spirit. Nowadays more than ever, living according to the perfect will of God is a true feat, so much so that these who make the choice are often compelled to stand against the society's influence. The men and women who succeed in doing so will nevertheless, at the end of their life, be hailed as heroes, because they have succeeded in not conforming themselves to values contrary to God, by firmly withstanding the negative hold society can sometimes have. When the time comes, they will realize the repercussions of their behavior in the natural world, but also in the spiritual world.

Through this book, I suggest you three pieces of advice that will help you in this approach to become a man or a woman according to the heart of God, and show thus the hero inside you. The first one answers the need of Man, who, to shape himself, is constantly looking for models he can refer to. In fact, in a world whose landmarks are challenged, in which the foundations and the traditional patterns that enabled peoples to become great nations, are being undermined, it is time to turn our looks to the perfect model that pleases God. The second one sheds light on some attributes it is fundamental to develop, so as to satisfy the heart of God and to influence our environment by making his will. Finally, the third one encourages us to act, by showing the Hero who lives in every born-again Christian, that is to say Jesus Christ.

ADVICE N°1

Modeling Jesus Christ
to please God's heart

Chapter 1
Every society needs to have models

"Don't let anyone look down on you because you are young, but set an example for the believers in speech, in conduct, in love, in faith and in purity." (1 Timothy 4:12)

On what grounds can we genuinely deem someone? Is it according to his charisma, his accomplishments, his values, his social status, his expression or to his being appreciated or not by others? What are the hints that enable us to assert that someone is good or bad, respectable or not?

Every one of us has his own criteria on which he relies to consider the other. They are so deeply rooted that they unconsciously influence the way we perceive things, people, and ourselves. We usually have the instinct of sizing people up depending on the first impression they give us. We generally make a judgment with criteria such as:

- The physical appearance: the height, the body shape, the face

- The clothing style: classic, sporty, formal office, preppy, streetwear

- The attitude: smiling, close-minded, haughty, distant, polite or not

- The distinctive features of identification to a social class: working-class, middle-class, executive, manager

- The way someone speaks, etc.

Our family, our education, our company, our professional setting, our age and our experiences have built the background through which we perceive and understand the people around us. Since that, it is extremely hard for our point of view to be neutral, for it greatly depends on these influences. Only once we have taken time knowing someone that we can be assured if our first impression really was right or not. By the way, you will surely admit on second thought that more than once, your first impression was wrong.

In our relationships, we adopt so to speak two kinds of attitudes. On the one hand, these who stay true to themselves and behave in the same way no matter who they are with. On the other hand, those who adjust their behavior and their language whether they consider themselves superior or inferior to the person they are with. Of course, the concept of superior and inferior is biased, since it depends on the way we consider ourselves. That is why you may see some people adopting a high-handed attitude towards men or women deemed inferior on a social level, and bend over backwards with other people deemed superior, because they are higher in the class system. If society likes to label, the Bible teaches us that all human beings are created equal, and you shall not judge others.

Indeed, only the One who searches the heart and examines the mind truly knows Man and what is deep inside of him. However, you really know someone only through his heart.

1 - Man needs models to shape his personality

Human beings naturally need to refer to a model to shape their personality. Yet, the modern world suffers in a growingly painful way from a lack of references. People generally take inspiration from a person endowed with some qualities and characteristics, or who has accomplished a significant thing that made them stand in awe. This person is admittedly not perfect; however, he is a source of inspiration for the people who know him intimately or vaguely. He makes them want to look like him. This desire comes from the admiration they have for him. They feel that, by acting like him, this will make them a better person, or at least the one they yearn to be. This need to have a model is not something new, it has existed since time immemorial. Plato, one of the first Western philosophers (428 BC), was Socrates's and Pythagoras's student. The prophet Elisha learnt from the prophet Elijah, Joshua from Moses, and the disciples of Jesus Christ drew inspiration from their master to keep spreading the message of the Gospel after his leaving and to demonstrate the power of the Kingdom of God through healings and miracles. Likewise, a large number of doctors, lawyers, farmers, nurses and teachers, tell you that they have chosen their job because it was a relative's or an acquaintance's.

This yearning is very strong among the youth, notably during the teenage years when building landmarks is crucial. In fact, just as a house has to be built on a solid foundation, a child needs landmarks to build his identity. When he watches the adult world, he discovers a range of profiles, and among them, some arouse his interest more than others. He needs to have a concrete representation of what he would like to become later, because this helps him to look to the future and to build his identity. That is the reason why the teenagers' bedrooms are filled with posters of their favorite singer or basketball player. The model plays a major role, because he is tremendously inspirational for some young boys or girls.

Sympathy and/or closeness can spur the choice for a reference. Usually, the first models are the parents. They teach their child how to think and behave, then it is the turn of the educational system, and then the media. The father and the mother are supposed to be the first examples from which the child will build his way of being. I mean "suppose to", because we know that unfortunately, it is not always necessarily so. Some children naturally copy their parents' acts, which brings them to become like them. Thereby, they adopt both their good and bad behavior. Others, when they grow up, recognize in their father and/or mother some specific attractive or repulsive aspects in their character, their behavior and their habits. So, they deliberately choose to adopt what they would like to copy, and put aside what does not suit them. However, for some people, some character traits may be so ingrained that they seem to control their life and shape what they become.

If you notice that some character traits keep lasting, or some incidents repeatedly happen with your family, generation after generation, you then have to search to make sure it is not a generational curse[1].

____

1. Generational curse: Misfortune that seems to recur like an endless circle, on a whole family, or on some members of a family, generation after generation. Medicine describes some pathologies as hereditary, but when we take time to understand, we can discover that it is actually about generational curses.

The choice of the reference can also be centered on people whom there is no direct contact with, just a sort of attraction. Some appreciate so much who they are and what they do that they even have the impression of knowing them. This lively interest makes them interested in them, to know more about them. This kind of relationship is generally formed between a fan and his favorite singer, athlete, star or actor. Even though they do not know one another directly, and they will probably never meet, yet the fan feels such a strong affection for him that he sometimes has the feeling that he knows him personally.

The expression of this desire to have someone we can refer to varies from one individual to the other. For some, this wish is so strong that they deliberately look for a person from whom they can learn and take inspiration, because they long for a deep change in their personal life, for getting some keys to succeed professionally (referred to as a mentor), or advice at the sentimental level or else. This need has grown bigger over the past few years, which explains that the personal development industry has soared. Others are not aware of having a model, even though they copy someone they greatly admire without thinking. Human beings tend to reproduce what they see, hence the need to have examples on which they can rely. There are, on the one hand, these who are influential, and, on the other hand, those who are influenced. However, it should be noted that influential people were once or sometimes are still influenced today.

In order to properly understand the reasons why a person is a model for one or more individuals, it is necessary to highlight three important elements: **his qualities, his characteristics and his accomplishments**. They can be seen cumulatively or not, within the person considered as the reference model.

2 - The three components that make someone a model

• Qualities

The word quality refers to the way someone is, either a good or a bad person. A model can be a person with good qualities, as a person with bad ones. In other words, it may be about a person valued for his kindness, his availability, his attentiveness, his disposition, as it can be about a person valued for his cynicism, his nastiness and his dishonesty. This can seem odd, right? But you know like I do that human beings are full of inconsistencies. Just like there are good qualities, there are bad qualities as well. The way each one of us judges them depends on who we are, because everybody has, depending on the way of thinking, his own frame of reference for what he considers a quality or a flaw in the other. He thus chooses the points he would like to see growing within him, by getting inspiration from a model.

Maybe you know the movie *Scarface*, in which Al Pacino embodies a contract killer who becomes a drug lord, and *Heat*, a movie about a truck robbery that turned out bad? Redoine Faïd, who became the number-one public enemy in France for many robberies and spectacular jailbreaks, confessed he was greatly influenced by these two feature films when he was younger. *Scarface*'s drug dealer and *Heat*'s robber became real heroes in his view, because he liked their charisma, their self-control and their smartness. He took inspiration from them to become himself a robber.

- **Characteristics**

The Cambridge dictionary defines a characteristic as: "*a particular quality or feature that is typical of someone or something*". It can be about physical characteristics: the size, the beauty, the strength; moral characteristics such as kindness, loyalty, bravery; or talent: dynamism, inventiveness and eloquence. Like quality, the characteristic may also be positive or negative. When the characteristic is a dominant trait, it strongly influences the attitude of the person in question. Attitude is fundamental in each and every one's life, for when it is good, it attracts favor and success, but when it is bad, it destroys relationships at last, which might lead to rejection, isolation and failure. When you understand this and you bring it at the scale of a neighborhood, a city or a country, you realize that a nation's general atmosphere depends on his inhabitants' and leaders' attitude.

Even today, Michael Jordan is considered the best basketball player ever, even though he put an end to his career in 2003. He was endowed with outstanding physical qualities, among which his jump. He would jump so high that his head would get well above the rim and he could remain suspended in air, whereas his opponents who tried to block him had already come back to the floor. With this characteristic, he earned the nickname of Michael Air Jordan, and he has become a model for millions of basketball players throughout the world.

- **The accomplishments**

Some people become inspirational models because of their accomplishment(s). They have done something significant, been successful in a specific field, and/or reached a certain reputation that draws the people's attention. It can be a work of art, a book, a movie, a sporting feat, the launch of a movement, an innovation, a success story, a heroic act, the defense of a cause, etc. Fascinated by what they have been able to do, some take inspiration from their background, hoping that they would become like them one day and accomplish something similar.

Gandhi contributed to the independence of India in 1947. His movement was uncommon because it was non-violent. His mode of action had such a resonance in the country and abroad that he was called the apostle of peace. Gandhi was inspirational to several liberation movements and civil rights activists in the world. The way he acted influenced great leaders like Martin Luther King. If Gandhi could see through such a change, it is mostly thanks to his personality. His movement did not succeed by mere chance then, but it rather had to do with who he was in his heart of hearts. His success is also due to the support of his close associates. The men and women who work in the shadow, and who too contribute to the success of a person, a work or a movement, must never be neglected, because behind every success hide people of worth.

3 - What about today?

When we take time to compare the criteria that used to enable someone to be popular with today's, we realize that in the age of social networks and reality TV, they have tremendously changed. While formerly, some qualities or having done something special was required, we see from now on ordinary people propelled to fame for no real reason except having successfully made a name for themselves. The social networks, TV shows and mainstream media have become experts at creating people out of the blue and making them so-called stars. The reputation they get and the image they or the media convey of themselves make them models. This is how the personality they convey and/or the way that has made them so popular become inspirational. Some would argue that the times have changed, I would rather say that standards are different, and consequently times.

The values ensuring a more or less balanced society, in which anyone can fit into society and live as he wishes, are being increasingly jeopardized. The heart of man and woman being devious by nature because of sin, they daily have to choose between their good or evil side. Respecting these values compels them to favor the best within themselves, rather than evil. But the loss of some norms has entailed their evil side to be emphasized, hence the rise of violence, immorality, injustice, corruption, in a word, of individualism. The impacts spread to all the layers of society, which accounts for the state of the world we live in. It is representative of Man's heart. If there are quite a number of reasons for that, it is also partly due to the losing of some reference models.

When parents fail in their role, when custodians of law, or people entitled with some responsibilities and a certain amount of authority, adopt an attitude that stands against requirements their function demand, when the media praise such and such celebrity's misconduct, when series, movies and video clips encourage inappropriate behavior, the ones and the others' minds eventually get used to that, and find it common. Mature people manage to put things into perspective, but youth find it fine, because they have only known that after all. There have always been men and women setting examples, but what makes them a model to emulate is the criteria, which have significantly changed over the years. Society in fact tries hard to put forward some models fitting with the trends, which necessarily brings about a shift in the appreciation of values, and a switch in the notions of good and evil.

Paul, the apostle wrote to his spiritual son Timothy: *"Don't let anyone look down on you because you are young, but set an example for the believers in speech, in conduct, in love, in faith and in purity"* (1 Timothy 4:12). Thus, we see that Paul considers as models people who pay attention to their words, their behavior, their love, their faith and their sanctification.

People look for models; qualities in one or accomplishments in another are inspirational. God has given us a perfect model. We will see in the following chapters that Jesus Christ is the reference model *par excellence*. He is perfect through his **qualities**, his **characteristics** and his **accomplishments**. Many find it hard to handle this idea, because consciously or not, they have put Him in the religious category only, which degrades the image they have of Him, and makes them feel like He is absolutely out of touch from what they can endure on a daily basis.

Jesus Christ has certainly not come to bring a new religion or philosophy, but He has come to bring life, and life in abundance. It is accessible to men and women who adopt the thought of God. By the way, when you observe the people who succeed with honesty and enjoy happiness, you notice that they implement to a certain extent His precepts, even if they sometimes do not notice it. Those who respect them benefit from the bound blessings, whereas those who transgress them experience disappointment, because the spiritual principles established by God are applicable to all men, whatever their beliefs. I would like to present to you in the next chapter, Jesus Christ, his life and his accomplishments, to understand why He is the only perfect model. Whoever models Jesus Christ is pleasant to the heart of God, because He is the only one who has unquestionably been agreeable to His eyes.

Chapter 2
Jesus Christ, the ultimate model

"And we all, who with unveiled faces contemplate the Lord's glory, are being transformed into his image with ever-increasing glory, which comes from the Lord, who is the Spirit." (2 Corinthians 3:18)

Jesus Christ is the most well-known character in all History, but He is also the One who has been, up to now, subject to many controversies. Talking about God is not problematic, but talking about Jesus provokes straight away tensions and disagreements. People living in a culturally Christian country have an idea of who He is, to a greater or a lesser extent, even if their knowledge remains superficial. Most of the people who know his story concede He had an exceptional life, however, rather fewer believe He really is the Son of God. This disbelief originates from the fact that He is seen as a simple prophet, a wise man or a man who has brought a new philosophy. The restrictive opinion they have of Him necessarily interferes with their understanding, because rationale cannot grasp divine. Nobody can actually understand the things of the Spirit, unless the Holy Spirit unveils them, because spiritual realities can be grasped only through revelation (1 Corinthians 2:11).

Revelation is the language of spiritual things; it is when the Holy Spirit unveils hidden things and makes them understandable to our conscience. Generally, the men and women who have the desire to understand and who open their heart have a way easier access to revelation than others. This is how people who had never believed before and who receive the revelation of God's mysteries, wonder afterwards how they did to disbelieve, because these things are from now on so self-evident for them.

1 - The life of Jesus Christ, a fulfilled life

One night, a Jewish leader called Nicodemus came to visit Jesus and told Him: *"Rabbi, we know that you are a teacher who has come from God. For no one could perform the signs you are doing if God were not with him."* (John 3:2). Despite this obviousness, the Pharisees, very strict religious people concerning the principles left by Moses the patriarch, did everything possible to kill Him. They finally reached their goal thanks to the betrayal of one of Jesus's twelves disciples, Judas, or at least this is what they thought. In fact, Jesus explained long before his death the way He would die, carefully specifying to his disciples that He chose to give his life to save mankind, through this confidence: *"The reason my Father loves me is that I lay down my life – only to take it up again. No one takes it from me, but I lay it down of my own accord. I have authority to lay it down and authority to take it up again. This command I received from my Father."* (John 10:17-18).

Jesus pushed his love to the extreme by dying on the cross, to redeem mankind's sins. No human being has ever lived or made a mark in History as He has. His charisma, his attitude, his teachings, his knowledge of God's mysteries, his accomplishments and his unconditional love have not only impacted society at the time, but are affecting to this day millions of men and women. Most people tend to confine Him solely to the religious sphere, because of the image that emerges in society, yet his role cannot be limited to that. His contribution impacts every aspect of earthly life, and even way beyond. Jesus Christ has revolutionized mentalities by bringing a wisdom that exceeds men's. He has taught things such as: *«Whoever wants to become great among you must be your servant."* (Matthew 20:26), *"Greater love has no one than this: to lay down one's life for one's friends."* (John 15:13), or *"For many are invited, but few are chosen."* (Matthew 22:14). Through his teachings, He would convey important principles like: humbleness, unconditional love or the importance of dying to oneself to let one's true nature come out. His precepts are timeless, for they match the living standards intended by God.

• **A prophetic birth**

One day, an angel named Gabriel appeared to Mary, the mother of Jesus. The angel told her that she found favor in God's sight, and that she would give birth to a son she will name Jesus. The angel added two statements: he told her who the child is, and what God had destined Him for. He told her: *"He will be great and will be called the Son of the Most High. The Lord God will give him the throne of his father David."* (Luke 1:32). Mary wondered how this could happen, in the sense that she had never known any man. The angel then explained to her that the Holy Spirit would overshadow her, and she would be pregnant. Joseph, her fiancé, on learning about her pregnancy, decided to secretly break up with her so as not to disgrace her. When he was about to do it, an angel appeared to him in a dream and revealed to him as well what God had destined for this child. The angel told him: *"She will give birth to a son, and you are to give him the name of Jesus, because he will save his people from their sins."* (Matthew 1:21). Jesus comes from the Greek *Iêsoûs*, which originates from the Hebrew *Yeshua* meaning: "The Lord is salvation". Christ comes from the Greek *Christos,* which means "anointed", and whose Hebrew equivalent is Messiah. The anointed is someone chosen by God through divine anointment. His name clearly expresses **who He is**: Jesus is the Messiah who has come to save men. In the Jewish culture at the time, the name was seldom chosen by chance, for it was supposed to define the person who bore it.

After a period of time, Mary paid a visit to Elizabeth, a relative. She was six months pregnant with John the Baptist, the future messenger of God. When Mary greeted her, the child in Elizabeth's womb leaped, and she was filled with the Holy Spirit (Luke 1:41). Elizabeth then said to Mary: *"Blessed are you among women, and blessed is the child you will bear! But why am I so favored, that the mother of **my Lord** should come to me?"* (Luke 1:42-43). The Spirit of God had just revealed to her the divinity of the child Mary was bearing.

Jesus was born in a manger, in Bethlehem. At his birth, an angel of the Lord appeared to shepherds who were nearby, and told them: *"Today in the town of David a Savior has been born to you; he is the Messiah, the Lord."* (Luke 2:11). Other angels then came to join Him, and gave glory to God. The shepherds went to the manger, and found the child, as the angel had told them. They then told Mary and Joseph, and the attendants, what had happened to them. A few days later, the parents went to the temple to present Him to the Lord. Simeon, a righteous and pious man on whom was the Spirit of God, had also gone to the temple that day, carried along by the Holy Spirit. He took the newborn in his arms and declared: *"Sovereign Lord, as you have promised, you may now dismiss your servant in peace. For my eyes have seen your salvation, which you have prepared in the sight of all nations: a light for revelation to the Gentiles, and the glory of your people Israel."* (Luke 2:29-32). A prophetess called Ann, who also attended the temple that day, was giving glory to God too, since the Holy Spirit had just revealed the child's identity to her.

In another place, in the East, wise men saw the child's star shine, and traveled to Jerusalem to see Him. On their arrival, they asked: *"Where is the one who has been born king of the Jews? We saw his star when it rose and have come to worship him."* (Matthew 2:2). King Herod, who knew about it, summoned the religious leaders to understand who Christ was, and where He was to be born. He also brought the wise men in, for them to tell him where the child was. Herod claimed he too would like to adore Him, but it was in fact a mere stratagem. The wise men found the child and his parents, and gave them presents. They went back home by another route, because an angel warned them not to reveal it to Herod. Joseph was also warned by an angel through a dream, urging him to flee to Egypt. When Herod realized that he had been tricked by the wise men, he became furious, and ordered to kill all the children aged two and less who were in Bethlehem and its surroundings. How is it that Herod feared such a young child? He dreaded what this newborn was destined for.

Thereby, it is clear that several people knew who the child was, because God had divulged it to them. He was similar to the children of his age, but He was second to none because He was the Son of God. The right time had to be expected, for Jesus of Nazareth to grow up and fully manifest his true identity.

- **A mysterious childhood**

The Bible gives us very little information about the childhood of Jesus, except for a very interesting event that happened when He was twelve years old. His parents and He had gone to celebrate Passover in Jerusalem, and on their way back his parents realized that He was no longer with them. They initially did not worry about his absence, thinking He was with the other members of the convoy. So, they returned to Jerusalem, and found Him in the temple discussing with the doctors of the law. The religious people were amazed by the knowledge of this young boy. His parents scolded Him, but He gave them a surprising answer: *"Why were you searching for me? Didn't you know I had to be in my Father's house?"* (Luke 2:49). Obviously, Jesus clearly knew from the start what He was here for.

- **An outstanding ministry**

On the day of the baptism of Jesus, when he came out of the water, the Holy Spirit descended on Him in the bodily shape of a dove, and a voice spoke from heaven: *"You are my Son, whom I love; with you I am well pleased."* (Mark 1:11). That day, God the Father, God the Son and God the Holy Spirit gathered for this unprecedented event. The Holy Spirit led Him straight away into the desert, where He stayed forty days and forty nights without eating. At the end of these forty days, the devil came to tempt Him, but he managed to stand firm. After a while, He went to a synagogue, on Sabbath day, and read from the book of Isaiah, in chapter 61:

> *"The Spirit of the Lord is on me,*
> *because he has anointed me to pro-*
> *claim good news to the poor. He has*

At the end of his reading, He sat down. While eyes were still upon Him, He declared: *"Today this scripture is fulfilled in your hearing."* (Luke 4:21). That day, Jesus publicly announced the purpose of his mission. He was thirty years old at the time. Although his ministry only lasted three years, He did extraordinary things no man had done before Him. He brought a new thought, the Kingdom of God's, He cast out devils, He healed sick people, He raised people from the dead, He multiplied food, He walked on the water, He changed water into wine, He calmed a storm, and so much more. However, despite all the good acts He did, his detractors wanted to harm Him, because of the growing number of people who would follow Him, and especially because He claimed He was the Son of God. It was hard for them to believe that this plain man, known by some as being the son of Joseph, the carpenter, was the Messiah, the much-awaited Savior. Israel being at the time under the domination of the Roman Empire, the people had probably supposed that their liberator would be a king in pomp and pageantry, or a military leader who would come to free them from their tyrant. Whereas they expected a physical liberation, they could not perceive in Jesus their Savior, for He came to bring them a completely different release: it was inner. It consisted in tearing the opaque veil that covered their understanding, and kept their thoughts in darkness. The depth of his messages aimed at destroying the false beliefs they had assimilated, so as to enlighten their minds and to free them from the power of darkness. The signs and miracles made it possible to testify that the Father was truly with Him.

There was a time when Man was really free and enjoyed immeasurable bliss, thanks to the intimacy between him and God. Unfortunately, it came to an end on the day he disobeyed Him. God told Adam: *"But you must not eat from the tree of the knowledge of good and evil, for when you eat from it **you will certainly die**."* (Genesis 2:17). He emphasized his warning by adding "certainly", to stress what would happen in case of disobedience. Adam and Eve gave in to the temptation in spite of everything, and ate from the forbidden fruit. By transgressing God's will, they drew death to them, as He had announced them. Many people are surprised they still lived after their deed, as if God had somewhat spared them. But actually, Adam and Eve did die on that day, but it was a spiritual death. It consists in living outside God's presence and will. Far from God, the human being's thoughts which used to be congruent with his Creator's, soon directed growingly towards evil. From then on, the devil took hold of him by corrupting his thoughts, because of the sin that had taken place in his heart.

The Hebrew word for sin is "chatta'th", which means miss the target. This word is also used to describe an archer missing his target. In the biblical context, it is then translated by not reaching the standard of holiness expected by God. Man has been created in the image of God, to glorify Him as a role on Earth. Yet, whenever an individual commits a sin, he gets away from God's holiness, and as a consequence, from God's will and perfect plan for his life. Obeying His prescriptions does enable him to draw closer to Him, by redirecting his life in Jesus Christ's direction.

It is when Adam and Eve missed the target (sinned) that violence, war, inequalities and sinfulness that destroy human beings nowadays were born. Means had then to be found to stop this vicious circle, and reconcile Man with his Creator. God Himself took on bringing a solution by designating his

Son, to liberate men and women from the power of sin, which relentlessly urges them to break his principles and his laws, and as a consequence to self-destruction. For this liberation to happen, a sinless person had to take on himself the sentence that fell on all mankind. The Son of God accepted this role of mediator[1] and redeemer[2], by leaving Heaven and by coming down on Earth as a simple man, as tells us the author of the Book of Hebrews:

> *"Therefore, when Christ came into the world, he said: Sacrifice and offering you did not desire, but a body you prepared for me; with burnt offerings and sin offerings you were not pleased. Then I said, here I am - it is written about me in the scroll - I have come to do your will, my God. First he said, sacrifices and offerings, burnt offerings and sin offerings you did not desire, nor were you pleased with them- though they were offered in accordance with the law. Then he said, Here I am, I have come to do you will. He sets aside the first to establish the second."* (Hebrews 10:5-9)

---

1. *"For* there is *one God, and one mediator between God and men, the man Christ Jesus; who gave himself a ransom for all, to be testified in due time."* (1 Timothy 2:5-6)
2. Redeemer: "Jesus Christ who, by his crucifixion, redeemed the human race and saved it from eternal death".

- **Risen from the dead**

One night, armed men came to arrest Jesus, and led Him by force the high priest's house. He had just been betrayed by Judas, one of his twelve disciples, for thirty silver coins only. They questioned Him in order to find a reason to condemn Him, because they were looking for a way to get rid of Him. The elders of the people, the chief priests and the scribes asked Him to say if He really was the Son of God. Jesus answered them: *"You say that I am."* (Luke 22:70). On hearing these words, the high priest tore his clothes, and they decided by agreement to put him to death. They brought Him to Pontius Pilate, and asked him urgently to sentence Him. This one questioned Him, but found no legitimate reason to deserve death. In the face of their stubbornness, he finally gave in. Jesus was nailed to the cross between two malefactors. Among those who attended the scene, many mocked Him and called Him names. Despite that, Jesus prayed his Father and told Him: *"Father, forgive them, for they do not know what they are doing."* (Luke 23:34). The Earth was covered by darkness for about three hours, then Jesus cried out: *"Father, into your hands I commit my spirit."* (Luke 23:46), and passed away. The veil of the temple tore from top to bottom, the ground quaked, tombstones opened, and several saints came back to life. A centurion acknowledged at that moment that this man was indeed the Son of God.

Three days after his death, Mary Magdalene went to the tombstone, and much to her surprise, she saw that the stone had been rolled, and that the sepulcher had been opened. While she was still wondering where his body could have been taken, she saw Him here, standing before her. Jesus was alive. He was resurrected, in accordance with what He had announced to his disciples. Death could not hold Him, because

He had not committed any transgression deserving death. He appeared later to his disciples, and to five hundred brothers (1 Corinthians 15:6), who testified He was well and truly alive.

Throughout the Old Testament, several prophecies had come to foretell the coming of the Messiah, some so far as to describe the way He would suffer to save mankind. After his death, some sections such as chapter 53 in the book of Isaiah, suddenly took on another dimension, because they accurately described everything that really happened. The precision of this chapter and the fact that it was written about seven hundred years previously, once again backs the evidence that Jesus is definitely the Savior of the world chosen by God.

2 - An extraordinary identity: Son of God

The people who were in contact with Jesus could not remain indifferent. They were mesmerized by his wisdom, moved by his love, surprised by his authority, enthralled by his miracles and his power. They mostly wondered who this man could be. One day, Jesus asked his disciples: *"Who do people say the Son of Man is?"* (Matthew 16:13). They answered Him that some thought He was a prophet, others a messenger, others John the Baptist or Elijah the prophet. He then asked them who He could be, according to them. Peter answered Him: *"You are the Messiah, the Son of the living God."* (Matthew 16:16). Jesus gave him at that moment a puzzling answer. He told him: *"Blessed are you, Simon son of Jonah, for this was not revealed to you by flesh and blood, but by my Father in heaven."* (Matthew 16:17). Jesus just revealed to them a mystery, by unveiling that only the Spirit of God can enable someone to recognize that He is truly the Son of God. God Himself testified several times to the filiation between Him and Jesus.

On the baptism of Jesus, a voice resonated in the sky and the attendants heard: *"You are my Son, whom I love; with you I am well pleased."* (Mark 1:11). A few days before his death, Jesus withdrew on a mountain with Peter, and He was transfigured before them. A cloud covered them, and a voice came: *"This is my Son, whom I love. Listen to him!"* (Mark 9:7). At another point, while Jesus was explaining to his disciples that He had come to suffer, they heard, resounding in the sky: *"I have glorified it, and will glorify it again."* (John 12:28).

One day, Jesus was having a discussion with Jews and the subject of Abraham arose. Jesus told them the following: *"Very truly I tell you, before Abraham was born, **I am**!"* (John 8:58). On hearing that, they became infuriated and tried to throw stones at Him. Abraham having lived about eighteen hundred years before Jesus Christ, they could not believe that Jesus had lived before Abraham. This statement equated to a blasphemy for them, because by saying **"I am"**, Jesus was making Himself the equal of God. The wording formulation **"I am"** directly referred to God, because it is the way He introduced Himself to Moses when He wished him to go to Egypt to free the children of Israel who were enslaved there. When Moses asked God how he had to present Him to the people, God answered him: ***"I am who I am"*** (Exodus 3:14). Jesus Christ and the Father are one, that is the reason why the Son of God told Philip, one of his disciples: *"Anyone who has seen me has seen the Father."* (John 14:9). The son of God is the Word, as we can see in the foreword of the first book of John:

"In the beginning was the Word,
and the Word was with God, and
the Word was God. He was with
God in the beginning. Through him

*all things were made; without him
nothing was made that has been
made"* (John 1:1-3)

The Word (the Son) had to be embodied, though, in order to get a body to come down on Earth to talk from God. Verse 14 of the book of John explains to us how this happened:

*"The Word became flesh and
made his dwelling among us. We
have seen his glory, the glory of the
one and only Son, who came from
the Father, full of grace and truth."*
(John 1:14)

A large number of terms are used in the Bible to describe the person of Jesus, and I would like to display some of them to you, to show you that Jesus **IS** before all things, and in Him all things hold together (Colossians 1:17). The Bible tells about Him that:

- **Jesus is the gate that gives access to the Father:** *"I am the gate; whoever enters through me will be saved. They will come in and go out, and find pasture."* (John 10:9)

- **Jesus is the way, He is the truth, He is the life:** *"I am the way and the truth and the life. No one comes to the Father except through me."* (John 14:6)

- **Jesus is the good shepherd:** *"I am the good shepherd. The good shepherd lays down his life for the sheep."* (John 10:11)

- **Jesus is the resurrection and the life:** *"Jesus said to her: I am the resurrection and the life. The one who believes in me will live even though they die (...)"* (John 11:25)

- **Jesus is the light of the world:** *"I am the light of the world whoever follows me will never Walk in darkness but will have the light of life."* (John 8:12)

- **Jesus is the bread of life:** *"I am the bread of life whoever comes to me will never go hungry and whoever believes in me will never be thirsty."* (John 6:35)

- **Jesus is the vine:** *"I am the vine you are the branches. If you remain in me and I in you, you will bear much fruit; apart from me you can do nothing."* (John 15:5)

- **Jesus is the image of the invisible God:** *"The son is the image of the invisible God, the firstborn over all creation."* (Colossians 1:15)

3 - A singular relationship with the Father

These few verses testify to who Jesus Christ is: **He IS**. He did not need to make miracles, deliverances and to cure the sick to be seen and loved by the Father, since the Father loves Him, because He IS. This is why, even before He did anything, God said about Him: *"You are my son whom I love; with you I am well pleased"* (Mark 1:11). And it is precisely because Jesus knows who He IS, that He has been capable of stepping aside to put forward his Father and give Him all the glory.

Understanding the life of Jesus, his intimate relationship with the Father, and his love towards all men, allows us to have a better understanding of the way each one of us is called to live. He is the ultimate model to follow, in the sense that He has made the perfect joy of his Father. He has loved his Father, loved the others, He has achieved the will of the Father, He has completed what He had come for, and for all of that, He has been welcomed in the sky with honors, by receiving the Name which is above all names.

Before doing anything for God, we have to discover beforehand who we are in Him. God loves us without us doing anything. He loves us simply because He is our Father and we are His children, at least for these who have accepted Him. Understanding our filiation with our Father completely changes the relationship we have with God. God is a lot more than our Creator; He is our Father. A Father wants the best for his children, He protects them, He fulfills their needs, He makes every effort to ensure their bliss. Our relationship with Him must in no case be the one of a servant to his master, nor a sinner's to a judging God, but it must be a child's to his Father. It is this relationship that Jesus has come to show to men, a son's relationship to his father.

When we understand that, we are no longer afraid of the future or of the troubles of life. We no longer feel strangers in the family of God and we stop begging in our prayers, because we know that we are children of God, and that God cannot leave us behind, simply because He loves us. When we behave towards God like his children and we love Him from the bottom of our heart, we restore the filial status that had been broken at the fall of Adam and Eve. God has not created us out of necessity but by pleasure, and we have to see Him as our Father so that this link be created again. The Holy Spirit comes to pour out the love for the Father into our hearts, so that we are able to love Him really. Without this love, no man or woman is able to love God deeply. Our heart must be the place where his presence always remains, the throne on which He can sit and reign on our life. This depends on us, on what we let into our heart, and particularly on what we put first. Someone according to the heart of God puts the Father first in his life, because he has received the revelation of his love.

Chapter 3
Jesus, a hero like no other

"You know how God anointed Jesus of Nazareth with the Holy Spirit and power, and how he went around doing good and healing all who were under the power of the devil, because God was with him."
(Acts 10:38)

For every presidential election, we generally witness the same scenario. The different contenders claim they have the solutions to the problems met by the country. They say they have a strategy to recover, to make it emerge from a slump and give it back its former glory. Once the elections are over, it will not be long before the program of the newly elected candidate will be the subject of critics and strikes of all kinds. Among the very people who supported him, many are disappointed and regret their choice. When a society is in danger, its residents tend to look for hope in men and women thought to be able to rescue them. Everybody is looking for a savior in some way, depending on the issue they are concerned with. Environmentalists want a leader who will save the planet; bankers, a financier who will fix the economy; the sick person, a doctor who will enable him to regain health. For others, it can be about saving their marriage, their job or their child out of delinquency. The person who will help them out will be welcomed as a savior, because he will have managed to solve an issue for which they had no solution.

The story of mankind is full of stories of men and women whose actions have marked their era in a particular way. The legacy they have left still has an echo today. Every era has witnessed the emergence of, or rather should we say has given rise to, a certain type of hero and heroine, depending on the social, historical, political or cultural situation, or on a specific event. **No human being is born a hero but he becomes one**. Likewise, no human being declares himself a hero, instead the others refer to him in this way. Society has always been somewhat fascinated by men and women who have achieved something significant, who have some cleverness, wisdom, or demonstrate a specific personality trait. Society needs to have heroes so as not to forget its history, to have inspirational models for the coming generations, and to always keep in mind that every human being hides in him something exceptional that just waits for the timely moment to come.

Among the great popular heroes in History, Jesus Christ does not figure on the list, even though He deserves so to a very large extent. He is a subversive hero who has overturned the foundations and the system of values established outside the will of God. His life has not only upset his contemporaries, but also the whole of mankind. He has saved millions of lives and still saves some, even today. His name is one of the most famous in the world, since his presumed date of birth is nothing other than the reference point of the Gregorian calendar. He has accomplished things that no other one did before, nor even after Him. Most of the historians and intellectuals categorize Him almost exclusively as a religious leader, a wise man or a prophet. However, He represents a lot more than that for the people who have truly understood who He is, the scope of his messages and his life, as well as his ultimate deed, which is the acceptance of his crucifixion. He is their model, their older brother, their advocate with the Father, their Savior, their Redeemer, He has given his life for mankind, He is the only one to have defeated death; in a word, He is their Hero. Jesus Christ has revolutionized the history of all mankind by bringing a thought from another world, a thought from the Kingdom of God. He is much more than a religious leader, a wise man or a prophet. He is the hero of all communities, because only He has been able to reconcile men with their Creator and to give them eternal life, by liberating them from the power of death and sin, and by tearing the veil that maintained them in darkness.

1 - Jesus has come to restore the sight to the physically and spiritually blind

After having fasted forty days and forty nights, Jesus went to the temple on Sabbath day, and He read the following passage:

> *"The spirit of the Lord is on me,*
> *because he has anointed me to pro-*
> *claim good news to the poor. He has*
> *sent me to proclaim freedom for the*
> *prisoners and recovery of sight for*
> *the blind, to set the oppressed free,*
> *to proclaim the year of the Lord's*
> *favor."* (Luke 4:18-19).

Jesus has said that He had come to proclaim liberation for the captives, however, at no moment we have seen Him lead a military riot against the Roman empire that dominated all the region at the time. We understand at this point that when He talked about captives, He referred to people who were ill and had unclean spirits, but not only. He was also talking about all the people locked in their way of thinking and prisoners of the devil's lies, simply because they did not know the truth. This is why He said to the Jews: "*If you hold to my teaching, you are really my disciples; then you will know the truth, and the truth will set you free.*" (John 8-31). All those who hear his Word and accept it in their heart are liberated, because his words are Spirit and life (John 6:63). Yet, *we know that where the Spirit of the Lord is, there is freedom* (2 Corinthians 3:17). Jesus is the Word made flesh, and each of his words gives life and faith in the spirit of the one who hears them. This is why the Bible tells us that: "*Consequently, faith comes from hearing the message, and the message is heard through the word about Christ.*" (Romans 10-17).

- **Emancipation by the truth**

In September 2018, Jean Botham, a young 26-year-old African-American, was killed in his apartment by Amber Guyger, a 31-year-old former police officer, who thought she was getting back home. When she saw the young man sitting in the living room, she shot him dead straight away. After a few seconds, she realized that she was not in her condo, but in the young man's. This tragic event moved a large proportion of the United States. On October 2, 2019, the trial was highlighted by a particular event that bewildered many, for Jean Botham's little brother said to the former policewoman that he forgave her, and he asked the judge if he could take her in his arms. In spite of this tragic accident, he found the strength to forgive his brother's murderer.

This story shows us well that when we have a bad perception of things, our certainties are necessarily distorted, and what we think being true, is actually not as true as it seems to be. Amber Guyger was 100% sure to be in her home, it was in a way "her reality". However, right after having committed this tragic deed, she realized that what she thought to be true, was actually not, and that is what unfortunately impaired her judgment. In other words, a lie, a mistake or incorrect information, can create a "wrong reality" which can become "our reality", if we believe it and accept it as true. Thus, a large number of men and women live in a kind of "virtual reality", because what they consider as true relies on elements, arguments or facts that are not. Every human being should look for the truth, so as not to make the mistake of passing by his life, because of the truncated image one can have of reality.

Jesus has presented Himself as being the way, the truth and the life. He is the only way leading to the Father, the truth that frees from the lies of the enemy, and the life that produces life in abundance. He has come to liberate the men and the women from all spiritual and intellectual blindness, by informing them of the truth. Truth undoes the power of lies, which alters our reality and the way we see and understand things. That is why Jesus said to his disciples: *"If you hold to my teaching, you are really my disciples. Then you will know the truth, and the truth will set you free."* (John 8:31-32). In my opinion, this verse is part of the most powerful passages of the Gospel, because it makes us understand how much the knowledge of the truth enables the liberation of the individuals, by rectifying them onto the reality of God. Hence the importance of reading the Bible regularly and particularly of meditating on it, that is to say going over some verses in our hearts until they get engraved in our hearts, and become our reality. Whenever we manage to seize the reality of a verse, we immediately have access to the promise that is bound to it. The more we know the Word of God, the more we walk in the victorious life in Christ, because our reality no longer relies on what we see with our physical eyes, but on what the Bible says. Jesus said to his disciples: *"Everything is possible for one who believes."* (Mark 9:23). Consequently, the more we believe in the Word of God, the more our intellectual boundaries are expanded, thanks to our inner growing faith in us. We no longer worry about knowing how God will handle things, but we rely on his Word, namely "With *your mouth you have promised and with your hand you have fulfilled it*" (1 Kings 8:24).

- **Freedom by changing the way of thinking**

The main message that Jesus has brought consisted in changing our way of thinking. When He began his ministry, He would repeat: *"Repent, for the kingdom of heaven has come near."* (Matthew 3:2). Other versions, like the Segond 21, read: "***Change your attitude***, *for the kingdom of heaven has come near.*" Put differently, Jesus has come to bring another way of thinking, He has come to change our perspective, so that our thoughts are from now on directed from the sky towards the Earth. It is sometimes a long and painful process, which occurs within us and, little by little, transforms us. But while you are persisting on, you will soon notice a change in the way you used to see and prioritize things, and the motivations that used to lead your life until now will be completely bowled over as well. That is the reason why, when his disciples asked Him to be taught how to pray, Jesus started the Lord's prayer by the following thing: "*Our father in heaven, hallowed be your name, **your kingdom come, your will be done, on earth as it is in heaven.**"* (Matthew 6:9-10).

This verse is an invitation for the Kingdom of God to be brought forth on Earth, for its laws, its principles and values may take part in the life of its inhabitants, so that they can enjoy the countless privileges they provide, one of them being freedom. So, the true liberty is only accessible to men and women who act with the thought of the kingdom of God, because it enables them to really understand who they are, and how the world is arranged. The people who discover their identity in Christ, no longer feel the need to follow the masses, not even to do something to exist. But they do all they can to become what God has planned from all eternity (Jeremiah 29:11).

Jesus has come to liberate the captives. It is the mandate He has left to his disciples, by telling them that in his name, they will drive out the demons, they will heal the sick, and they will raise the dead (Matthew 10:8). The born-again Christians and full of the Holy Spirit have received both authority (the name of Jesus), and power (the Holy Spirit), to act on Earth, and they in turn, to liberate the captives as Jesus did. In various places, we increasingly often witness miraculous healings or liberations. The Kingdom of God is moving forward, and He is looking for men and women to strengthen his army. The war is not against flesh and blood, that is to say men, but against principalities, dominions and evil spirits in heavenly places, as described in this verse:

"Put on the full armor of God, so that you can take a stand against the devil's schemes. For our struggle is not against flesh and blood, but against the rulers, against the authorities, against the powers of this dark world and against the spiritual forces of evil in the heavenly realms." (Ephesians 6:11-12)

Dominions[1] are forces influencing nations, cities and territories. **Authorities** are powers influencing governments, in particular on decision-making leading to the voting of some laws. If you notice the same kind of laws voted at the same time in several countries, it is no coincidence, for these powers take an active part in the establishment of a new world order, in order to influence and control as many as possible. The **princes of the kingdom of Darkness** influence human beings by arousing false religions and doctrines, and by spurring them on to occult practices. **Evil spirits** incite men to sin and to commit all sorts of atrocities: sexual perversion, crimes, addictions…

These evil spirits interfere with the business of the human beings, by influencing countries, regions and cities, with false doctrines, beliefs, values and mores at the opposite of God's. Their goal is to corrupt the heart of Man, so as to control his way of thinking. Very few people realize it because of strongholds firmly fixed in their mind, and influence their perception of reality. It is important to be aware of that, to be able to struggle against all kinds of strangleholds which lock up individuals. War must be led against all forms of emotional limitations (fear, anger, stress, depression, wounds of the soul), physical (diseases), or even intellectual (education, philosophy, science), since some ideologies can imprison people by preventing them to see themselves as God has really created them.

Fortunately, on the cross of Golgotha, Jesus Christ has defeated the power of all those evil forces, and He has destroyed the conviction placed on all who trust Him:

––––––––––––––––––

1. *"Power behind the scenes"*, Archbishop Nicholas Duncan-Williams, 2014. *"Understanding your spirit world"*, John Mumba, 2014.

2 - The destruction of the power of death and sin

Jesus Christ has come to liberate the men from the power of sin, by destroying the power of darkness. When dying on the cross, He went down to Hades, but death could not retain Him, for He had perfectly respected all the Mosaic Law, by committing no fault whatsoever. He could not rationally stay in this place for sinners only, since the fall of Adam and Eve. Several passages in the Scriptures show us that through his death, Jesus Christ has annihilated the power of death by taking back the keys of death and of Hades:

51

might break the power of him who
holds the power of death — that is,
the devil — " (Hebrews 2:14)

While religious people were delighted about his death, little did they suspect that behind this act was the liberation of all mankind from the power of death. Satan too was exulting for having defeated the Son of God, until the moment when he saw Jesus claiming the keys of Hades. The cross is the crux of Christianity, it marks a turning point in mankind's whole history, because it marks the definitive withdrawal of the devil, who had no other choice than to give Him the keys. Thus, anyone who puts his life in the hands of Jesus Christ, also enjoys the benefits of his victory:

"When you were dead in your sins and in the uncircumcision of your flesh, God made you alive with Christ. He forgave us all our sins having canceled the charge of our legal indebtedness, which stood against us and condemned us; he has taken it away, nailing it to the cross. And having disarmed the powers and authorities, he made a public spectacle of them, triumphing over them by the cross." (Colossians 2:13-15)

By presenting Himself before the Father, Jesus showed Him his own blood to redeem the sins of mankind. This act is similar to the practice made by the main priest, who would present the blood of animals before God to <u>cover</u> the sins of the people, in the Old Testament (Leviticus 4:27-29). But to remove the sins of men, only the pure and perfect blood of

Jesus Christ could be presented before the Father. God being Holy, the blood of Jesus Christ, which is pure, had to purify and sanctify men for them to gain access to his presence and receive eternal life, as the author of the Epistle to the Hebrews outlines it so well: *"Therefore, brothers and sisters, since we have confidence to enter the Most Holy Place by the blood of Jesus."* (Hebrews 10:19). Jesus was given full authority in Heaven and on Earth (Matthew 28:18), and the Name that is above every name (Philippians 2:9). He restored to men the authority that Adam and Eve had given up to Satan, by having believed his lie and placed themselves this way under his authority. Consequently, everyone who accepts Jesus as Lord and personal Savior has the right to be forgiven his sins. He has nothing in particular to do, except for believing, since salvation is given by grace (Ephesians 2:8).

His ministry does not end after his leaving, because He is still alive today, and keeps revealing Himself to men and women through his Spirit. People who yearn for a deep change at some point of their lives, and who had a personal encounter with Him are countless. They witness that not only He is alive, but He has also completely upset their existence. Someone who pleases the heart of God is someone who, in the manner of Jesus Christ, endeavors to liberate the captives from all kinds of oppression, be they physical, spiritual or emotional. It cannot be done by our own might, nor even by our power, but by the Holy Spirit (Zechariah 4:6).

Chapter 4
Walking the way of Jesus

"For those God foreknew he also predestined to be conformed to the image of his Son, that he might be the firstborn among many brothers and sisters." (Romans 8:29)

One night, Judith asks friends to pray for her, so that she may be completely cured from her disease. She has suffered for several years from multiple sclerosis. While the group is praying for her, the Holy Spirit reveals to one of the brothers that something impedes in the way of their prayers. The latter feels at the bottom of his heart that she needs to forgive someone. He raises the question and asks her if there is someone in particular, she has to forgive. On hearing these words, Judith starts crying. She will later explain that she had been married for a short while, but she separated because her marriage went really bad. After this separation, her heart was invaded by anger and hatred towards her former husband. Some time later, the disease appeared. When listening to her story, they realized that the absence of forgiveness prevented their prayers to rise up to the throne of God. Judith was not able to forgive that day, because the pain was still way too sharp. But she asked God to give her the strength, and she made it a long time later. Meanwhile, the disease swept over to such an extent that she was likely to lose her sight. Despite the diagnoses of the doctors, she put her faith in God, and God totally healed her.

This story tells us what should be Christian life: a visible display of the power of God. By leaving his disciples, Jesus told them: *"Very truly I tell you, whoever believes in me will do the works I have been doing, and they will do even greater things than these, because I am going to the Father."* (John 14:12). The healings, the liberation, the emotional and spiritual restorations, have certainly not come to an end with the leaving of Jesus. He gave to his disciples, as well as all those who would commit themselves to follow Him afterwards, power and authority to carry on what He has started. He left to us several instructions, such as:

> *"I have given you authority to trample on snakes and scorpions and to overcome all the power of the enemy; nothing will harm you."*
> (Luke 10:19)

> *"And these signs will accompany those who believe: In my name they will drive out demons; they will speak in new tongues; they will pick up snakes with the hands; and when they drink deadly poison, it will not hurt them at all; they will place their hands on sick people, and they will get well."*
> (Mark 16:17-18)

1 - Manifest Christ in character and in work

The responsibility falling on men and women who have made the choice of following Jesus is to model Him, so that the legacy He has bequeathed to them does not vanish, but remains until He comes back. Healing the sick, chasing demons and raising the dead are part of the mission that Jesus has given to his people (Matthew 10:8), and even if physically absent, He is nonetheless present in the heart of the believers through faith. Here and there, miraculous healings are heard of more and more often, even though this is not necessarily covered in mainstream media, which prefer suggesting that Christianity is merely a lifeless religion. And when they decide to make a report, they purposely choose a weird church, or use a sarcastic tone to discredit a whole community. Religion is a set of laws and principles to which its members submit, but TRUE Christianity should be characterized by the life of the Spirit. In fact, Christians are no longer under the law, but they must be driven by the Holy Spirit. The Holy Spirit liberates the captives by bringing a mental, emotional, physical, spiritual and even financial freedom. He restores the soul, heals the inner injuries, brings peace, and pours out the love of God into the hearts. For this process to be complete, He must "pull us out" from conformism and of the culture of society. However, the effort is worth it, because it enables us to realign ourselves with the person we truly are, and those who manage to do it are then brought back to the initial position that God had planned for them, before the creation of the world. At that point, they leave the stage of mere believer or half-hearted Christian, to enter the stage of intimacy. They no longer behave as simple servants, but as friends of God.

- **A price to pay to have the character of Christ**

One day, I was on the phone with my friend Pascal, who is in the United States, and he told me something very interesting about the importance of paying the price, to have the character of Christ. Here is what he said to me: *"The price to pay will never replace the price that Christ has paid, but the price we pay enables us to fully understand through faith the price **He** has paid. The mistake of religion is to make us believe that the price we pay can replace the price **He** has paid."*

Why is the expression "pay the price" used? Because precious things have a high value, and they commonly demand a superior sacrifice from us. Only those who have a thirst for experiencing more things with the Father and the Son will be ready to pay the price. This thirst can come either from the Holy Spirit, or from a deep frustration on noticing the big difference between what the Bible says and what they live on a daily basis. It may also originate from the fact that they are surrounded with people who also actively seek God, or from people who have managed to nurture a deep intimacy with Him. On seeing what they experience, the way God talks to them and uses them, as well as the fruit they bear, you too feel like experiencing the same thing. Nobody can make it through his own powers, the Holy Spirit gives us the ability to do it, even if He needs to find a man or a woman whose heart is willing. Someone who is ready to put aside everything trivial, to let the first place to God. God observes us, and watches what we are ready to give up to have Him, and Him only. For some, it can consist in a toxic relationship, a bad habit, a bad trait, or all sorts of entertainments that take up all your free time, such as spending hours in front of the television, the computer or on the phone, whereas you could shorten this time to spend more of it in his Presence. The Holy Spirit will hardly ever force your hand, except if it is for the sake of your life. He generally creates desires, gives ideas or a direction, but He needs the person to get along with his will to be able to work in and through him.

In general, it is in quietness that God likes to reveal Himself to people, and bring them into a completely different dimension, so much so that his presence becomes increasingly true and palpable. Quietness is not so much about the physical place, even if this is very important, but you know as well as I do that you may be alone in your bedroom, and be overwhelmed by all kinds of thoughts, or constantly disturbed by phone calls or texts. It is about having some peace and quiet in your heart and in your thoughts, by putting aside all the daily worries, to focus your attention on Him, and Him only. This way, you can as well be in your car or on a crowded train, and yet be connected to the heart of God, because you have learnt to find quietness within yourself, and be in communion with Him. Your spirit is the place where you are one with God, and it is in quietness that you will perceive, little by little, the sweet voice of the Holy Spirit.

While you learn how to spend time in the presence of God, your faith will no longer be solely based on what you have read and heard, but on what you have personally seen and experienced with God, that is to say the revelation you have from Him presently. Your various experiences will strengthen your faith, so much so that it will become unwavering. From now on, His presence for you is so outstanding that you make every effort to keep it, and never to be lost. Now you know what pleases God and what saddens Him, what attracts His presence and what drives it away. You are careful about the way you speak, you check the thoughts that take up your intellect, you are mindful of what you let in your heart, you refuse arguments, you beg for pardon as soon as you have committed a wrongdoing, you make every effort to remain in love and express it. By the way, all these things allow you to have access to his intimacy. As you come closer to God, the Holy Spirit highlights the evil things hidden in the different rooms of your heart. For some, it might be about anger, vanity, selfishness or hypocrisy. For others, about a need for acknowledgement that is generally linked to a lack of self-confidence, or to conceit that pushes us into proving to others that we are better than them. For still others, it may be a matter of emotional wounds due to an intricate family background, of physical or emotional violence during childhood or at an adult age, or, as noted earlier, of a breakup that went really bad.

Maybe you think you are better than the others? You consider yourself more intelligent, more understanding, stronger, more attentive, kinder, quicker to give help? While you are striving to get closer to God, all kinds of strange feelings are overwhelming your thoughts and your emotions, so that you can feel unworthy and undeserving of his love. It is because the Holy Spirit lays your heart bare, so that you can see yourself as you really are, without any mask or any sham. Facing the mirror of your soul, you realize how much you need God, and his action in your life, to free you from all these things that have erected an invisible wall between Him and you. In a way, this separation symbolizes everything that keeps you away from Him, and prevents you from getting in his intimacy. It can deal with anger, slander, jealousy, immodesty, lies, rebellion, greed. Every brick of this wall must fall, to get full access to his presence, and for you to truly become yourself. The human being really discovers who he is, and what he has been created for, only before his Creator. The Holy Spirit can then begin his work of deconstruction with this repentant heart, to remodel the vessel of honor that you are for God. God is the potter and you are the clay. Your passing in His hands is necessary for

Him to give you back your true shape, because the ups and downs of life and the way the world functions have distorted you.

It reads in the Bible that: "*But whoever is united with the Lord is one with him in spirit.*" (1 Corinthians 6:17). The Greek word for bind is *kollao*, which means: to tie firmly, or to cement. The notion of "cementing" is very interesting, because it expresses a meld between two elements, so that they give form to only one at the end. It is true that those who are born again are a single spirit with God, because the Holy Spirit dwells in their spirit. However, how many people are truly ONE with God? How many have one same voice, one same thought, one same heart with Him? This is exactly the dimension to which God calls every one of us. However, it is not accessible to all, because it is restricted only to those who are ready to pay the price, to people who cannot be satisfied with an average Christian life. This is how the apostles lived at their time, and this is what is experienced by men and women who wish God to reveal to them his secrets and to talk to them face to face.

• **A price to pay in the prayer**

One day, Jesus said to the Jews that *He can do nothing by himself; He can do only what he sees his Father doing* (John 5:19). He also said that *He did not speak on his own, but the Father who sent Him commanded him to say all that He has spoken* (John 12:49). There was such a unity between Jesus and his Father, that absolutely everything that Jesus said was the expression of the thought of the Father, and everything He did was the manifestation of the will of God. This perfect harmony stemmed from the fact that Jesus was totally submitted to the Father. This is why Jesus answered Philip who wished to see God: *"Anyone who has seen me has seen the Father"* (John 14:9). Jesus was both 100% man and 100% God, but He lived as a simple man, because He had to overcome sin as man.

It is after a whole night of prayer that Jesus chose his disciples, and all who touched Him were healed, because a force came out of Him (Luke 6:12-19). It is after a time of prayer in the garden of Gethsemane that He found the strength to brave the terrible ordeal of the cross, and an angel came from the sky to strengthen Him (Luke 22:43). On seeing the healings, the numerous miracles, and on hearing his teachings, the disciples asked Him one day to be taught how to pray, because they had understood that all of that was only possible thanks to his life spent in praying.

This observation must bring every one of us to realize how important prayer is. If the Son of God, who perfectly knew the Father, needed to pray, even more so do the believers need to devote themselves to it as well. Prayer is in no case a religious exercise whose goal is to have a good conscience before God or for some, to appear to men. It is a dialog, a communication between God and his creation. It is not an option either, because it is the only way to develop a real intimacy with the Father. It is in quietness that the Father reveals Himself to you to a larger extent, when you focus your attention on Him, you speak to Him, and you take time to listen to Him. Whereas you expect Him to talk to you, He will certainly answer you in one way or another, as shows us this verse: *"You will seek me and find me when you seek me with all your heart."* (Jeremiah 29:13).

When you pray, it is important to rely on the Word of God, to be sure that God will pay attention to your prayer, and will act. If you are ill, you must find one or several verses that deal with recovery, such as: *"But he was pierced for our transgressions, he was crushed for our iniquities; the punishment that brought us peace was on him,* **and by his wounds we are healed.** *"* (Isaiah 53:5). If you go through particularly difficult moments, you can find hope in verses like: *"The righteous person may have many troubles, but the LORD delivers him from them all."* (Psalms 34:19). If you go through a situation you do not understand, you can remember that: *"And we know that* **in all things God works for the good of those who love him**, *who have been called according to his purpose."* (Romans 8:28). God may step in when you use his Word, because his Word commits Him, and we know that *God is not human, that he should lie* (Numbers 23:19). But I want to specify once again that our prayers must be presented before God with a sincere heart, and be inspired by the Holy Spirit.

- **The Bible**

The Bible contains all the life situations regarding human beings. It has all the answers to questions that men can ask. It is not a mere book that tells stories. The Bible was admittedly written by men, but under the inspiration of God: *"All Scripture is God-breathed and is useful for teaching, rebuking, correcting and training in righteousness, so that the servant of God may be thoroughly equipped for every good work."* (2 Timothy 3:16). It is a letter left by God for men to answer their existential questions, understand the reasons for their presence on Earth, grasp how much they need Him, encourage them to look for and discover who He is and how much his love is boundless. It is a message left for all mankind, to remind generations that men are not due to an accident, but they were rather desired by God, and created in his image and his likeness. It is a will left by a Father to his children, which includes the promises and legacy He has bequeathed them. It is an open door to eternity, showing men that there is a life after death. It is a light which illuminates the spirit of Man and puts him back into his true identity. This Word is living, it has become flesh, and it has been manifested in Jesus Christ (John 1:14).

The more you develop the habit of reading the Bible and the more the teachings, principles, wisdom and revelations come to "update" the software of your thoughts. They destroy everything that used to tie you to your former nature, which is now groundless, in order to substitute them by thoughts, convictions and feelings that, from now on, correspond to your new nature. As soon as someone gives his life to Christ, he immediately becomes a new creature: *"If anyone is in Christ, the new creation has come: the old has gone, the new is here!"* (2 Corinthians 5:17). This transformation is made possible thanks to the immediate regeneration of his spirit, by the Holy Spirit. However, his soul remains unchanged, which explains that his habits, his thoughts, his convictions and his behavior remain the same. The renewal of his thoughts, particularly through meditation on the Word, prayer, teachings, understanding his identity in Christ, fraternal communion and the relationship he will develop with God, will deconstruct little by little his way of thinking, which was tied to his former nature and locked him up in the world system. He can then build his new identity on relying on a sound and fair basis this time, that is to say thoughts, convictions, principles and values in connection to the Kingdom of God.

Pastor Derek Prince remained bedridden for a year in the military hospitals in Egypt during the Second World War, because of a skin disease that doctors were unable to heal. To recover, God showed him a way in Proverbs 4:20-22: *"My son, pay attention to what I say; turn your ear to my words. Do not let them out of your sight, keep them within your heart; for they are life to those who find them and health to one's whole body."* As a newly converted philosopher, whenever he heard about healing, he only thought about spiritual healing, because, according to him, God did not worry about the body. When he read: "the health of the whole body", he understood that God had provided the whole body with health. So, he decided to take the Bible as a medical prescription, that is to say by reading it morning, midday and evening. On meditating on this passage, he drew four instructions, which he followed, such as the indications you can find on a medicine bottle. This way, after about four months, he completely recovered in Khartoum, Sudan, in an unhealthy place and where the temperature is often around fifty degrees.

- **Faith**

Many people think they can reach the heart of God through their deeds. By the way, it is the mistake that most religions make. God is only accessible through faith, and He Himself places it in the hearts. No human effort whosoever can make an individual fair before God. That is the reason why the coming on Earth of the Messiah was necessary, so that through his sacrifice on the cross, all the men who believe in Him be justified. Since Jesus has said: "It is finished", there is nothing to be done, except for believing in this promise, to grasp everything bound to it. The born-again people are heirs of God and co-heirs with Christ, thanks to the work on the cross (Romans 8:17), and they benefit from all spiritual blessings in the heavenly realms (Ephesians 1:3). However, it is necessary to dwell in Christ.

One day, Jesus said: *"Remain in me, as I also remain in you. No branch can bear fruit by itself; it must remain in the vine. Neither can you bear fruit unless you remain in me."* (John 15:4). As long as the branch is part of the tree, it can bear fruit. The branch has no effort to make, except for remaining connected to the tree so as to receive its life and this way to bear fruit. Prayers, fasting and sacrifices can in no way give us something we already had from Christ, through the cross. These actions enable us to strengthen our faith, in order to have a greater revelation from God, and thus to get closer to Him. They also give us the power to achieve his work, but it can be efficient only if there is faith.

In the epistle of the Hebrews, chapter 11, verse 6, it is written: *"And without faith it is impossible to please God, because anyone who comes to him must believe that he exists and that he rewards those who earnestly seek him."* (Hebrews 11:6).

Faith is the prevalent element to walk in the steps of Jesus Christ, because our faith activates the power contained in the Holy Scriptures. Without faith, the Bible remains a mere book telling stories, but with faith, it takes a completely different dimension, because it becomes the genuine Word of God. Yet, the Word of God is living, powerful and active (Hebrews 4:12). When God speaks, his words produce an action or a reaction, because each of his sentences contains life. It is through faith in the Word of God that the sick people are healed, the devils are cast away, the impossible becomes possible, and the sky comes down on Earth. It is through faith that every one of us is called to walk, so that the heavenly realities may show in our daily life. Knowing the Word is a powerful weapon, dreaded by the enemy of our souls, since when we pronounce the Word with faith, each of our words has the same impact as if Jesus pronounced them. This is why the Bible tells us the following thing about the words pronounced by God: *"So is my word that goes out from my mouth; it will not return to me empty, but will accomplish what I desire and achieve the purpose for which I sent it."* (Isaiah 55:11).

2 - Deepening one's knowledge of God

• Developing one's communion with God

God speaks through his Word, but there are also other means through which He communicates with his children. He speaks through dreams, as we can see in the book of Job:

> *"For God does speak - now one*
> *way, now another - though no one*
> *perceives it. In a dream, in a vision*
> *of the night, when deep sleep falls*
> *on people as they slumber in their*
> *beds."* (Job 33:14-15)

God also speaks through visions, that is to say you are awake, your eyes can be closed or open, but you perceive an image or a scene in your spirit. Sometimes you can think that it is only your imagination, but God can use this means to relay a message to you.

In 2016, I was in a church in California, with a prophet friend to whom God speaks a lot through visions. When getting out of the service, we came across a group of young women. My friend said to one of them: *"I can see music notes all around you, and I can see you playing the guitar!"*. The girl was seized at once by the Holy Spirit, and her friends supported her so that she would not fall. As we were trying to understand what was going on, one of her friends explained to us that she was indeed a singer and that she played the guitar. How could he know? He got this piece of information from the Holy Spirit. He kept going on by prophesying over her life, because God had given to him specific words for this woman. God can then speak through prophetic words, by inspiring specific words concerning someone.

God also speaks through thoughts, generally using the little voice of our conscience. When you are not used to it, it is very difficult to make a difference between your own thoughts and the ones that are inspired by the Holy Spirit. But over time, you start discerning them little by little. When a thought lightens up your mind, gives you a piece of information about which you did not think a few minutes earlier, passes on a piece of advice or wisdom superior to yours, confirms you a doubt or a certainty you had, it is very probably a thought inspired by God. This role falls to the Holy Spirit who, as we have seen before, gives you the thought of God.

Has it never happened to you to make a car journey, and as you fall into a huge traffic jam, you say to yourself that you should never have taken this route, because a little inner voice had warned off it? Or else, you meet someone, and while most of the people praise him, you do not know why, but something in him disturbs you. Sometimes you even blame yourself for having this kind of thoughts. But much later, when a specific incident happens, and his true face appears out, that you realize that you were right. You understand at this point that this sense did not originate from you, but from God, who communicates a lot through intuition.

The author Francis Myles[1] explained during a conference in Brussels that many people miss the voice of God, and end up finding themselves in trouble by their own fault. He exemplified that with an accident that happened to him when he was in South Africa to attend a conference. At the end of the day, while he was driving back, a thought advised him to turn left. He did not see the point of taking that route, since this detour would extend his route for about thirty minutes. He

---

1. *"The Spirit of divine interception"*, Dr. Francis Myles, Kingdom House Publishing, 2017.

went on his way, when on reaching a crossroads he was hit by a truck. When getting out of the car, he was badly surprised to note that it was thoroughly destroyed. The vehicle was not his, somebody had lent it to him, and to top it all, the truck had no insurance and the driver had no driving license. Establishing a report was consequently impossible. At that moment, he bitterly regretted not having listened to his sense, because he knew that God had warned him.

• **The people who walk with God**

The Bible tells us about some people whose relationship with God was so privileged that God would **walk** with them. The use of this formulation is very strong, since it reveals true harmony and closeness. In fact, the Scriptures tell us about this topic: *"Do two walk together unless they have agreed to do so?"* (Amos 3:3). Walking alongside someone implies progressing at the same pace, going in the same direction and being in perfect tune. Several men of the Old Testament have been graced with walking with God. What was so special about them in comparison with others? I would like us to observe a few of them, to understand that our ultimate quest must be to walk with Him too, to make sure that He is well and truly by our side.

• **Adam and Eve**

At the beginning, the Creator would regularly go down to the Garden of Eden and talk with Adam and Eve. One day, as usual, He came to them, but this time they hid, because they had just disobeyed his recommendations: *"Then **the man and his wife <u>heard</u> the sound of the LORD God as he <u>was walking</u> in the garden in the cool of the day**, and they hid from the*

LORD God among the trees of the garden." (Genesis 3:8). The New Segond Bible study supplies us with a very interesting detail about this passage. The footnote in fact indicates this: "The word corresponding to *voice* can also mean *noise*. It can also be understood as: the sound (of footsteps) of the Lord." This comment hints that God would <u>walk</u> with Adam and Eve, until the day when their relationship was broken. This same expression is found again: "*sound of footsteps*", about King David and God.

One day, as David was about to fight the Philistines, he asked God beforehand to know whether he had to assault them or not. God gave him this answer: "*As soon as you hear* ***<u>the sound of marching</u>*** *in the tops of the poplar trees, move quickly, because that will mean* **the LORD <u>has gone out</u> in front of you** *to strike the Philistine army.*" (2 Samuel 5:24). God's presence alongside David would without a doubt guarantee his success. Since then, it is much easier to understand how this mere shepherd succeeded in everything he undertook. Why did God walk with Adam and Eve, and David? Adam and Eve were perfect, flawless, but unfortunately, it came to an end on the day when they disobeyed. Their closeness with the Creator stopped, because of the sin that entered their heart. As for King David, he was far from being perfect, but the Bible tells us he was a man according to the heart of God though, for the state of his heart would make him pleasant to the eyes of God.

- **Enoch**

The Bible tells us about a man named Enoch who also walked with God. The Old Testament does not really give us any information about him, but what draws our attention is that not only did he <u>walk</u> with God, but he also had a very particular fate:

> *"After he became the father of Methuselah, Enoch* **<u>walked</u> faithfully with God 300 years** *and had other sons and daughters. Altogether, Enoch lived a total of 365 years.* **Enoch walked faithfully with God***; then he was no more, because God took him away."* (Genesis 5:22-24)

The writer of the Epistle to the Hebrews gives us a little more details concerning this mysterious man, and the reason why God abducted him without him seeing death: *"By faith Enoch was taken from this life, so that he did not experience death: "He could not be found, because God had taken him away." For before he was taken, he was commended as one who pleased God."* (Hebrews 11:5). On reading this verse, we can see that Enoch was so pleasant in the eyes of God, that He took him away before he reached the end of his life. Enoch walked three hundred years with God, and he was abducted at the age of three hundred and sixty-five. A quick deduction enables us to understand that Enoch began walking with God at the age of sixty-five. During these first sixty-five years, Enoch must certainly have learnt to know God, and from this friendship was born the fact that they progressed together and that God decided to abduct him.

- **Moses**

Moses is also one of the men who <u>walked</u> with God. The Bible relates us that *"The LORD would speak to Moses face to face, as one speaks to a friend."* (Exodus 33:11). What a statement! One day, Moses questioned God to know who would come with him to lead the people. The subsequent dialog clearly proves the closeness existing between them:

> *"The LORD replied, "**My Presence will <u>go</u> with <u>you</u>**, and I will give you rest." Then Moses said to him, "**If your Presence does not go with us,** do not send us up from here. How will anyone know that you are pleased with me and with your people unless you go with us? What else will distinguish me and your people from all the other people on the face of the earth?" And the LORD said to Moses, "**I will do the very thing <u>you</u> have asked, because I am pleased with <u>you</u>** and I know you by name." Then Moses said, "Now show me your glory.""* (Exodus 33:14-18).

Let us have a closer look at this text to understand how deep it is. God told Moses: **"*My Presence will go with you*"**. In other words, God tells him that He in person will accompany him, not a man. Instead of answering that He will walk with the people, God reassures Moses by telling him that He will walk by his side. Instead of being delighted with that, Moses tries to bring the discussion into focus by specifying that it is not only about him, but about the people as well. That is why he answers the following thing: **"*If your Presence does not go*</u>**

*with **us***". At that point, God gave him a surprising answer: "***I will do the very thing you have asked, because I am pleased with you***".

It might be thought that God answers completely off the point at first glance, but on studying this passage, we understand that God would walk with the people thanks to Moses. It is important to precise that before this discussion, the anger of God was set on fire against the people and He wanted to destroy them, because they had made a golden calf to worship it (Exodus 32). Fortunately, Moses managed to soothe God's anger. The existing intimacy between God and Moses was one of the reasons why God would lead this people despite everything. The people would benefit from the favor of God through the relationship God had with their leader. When God says to Moses: "*I will do the very thing you have asked*", Moses hurried to answer: "*Now show me your glory*" Moses asks one of the rarest things that can be for human beings: to see the glory of God. **Because seeing the glory of God is seeing God Himself.**

This passage helps us have a better understanding of the reason why some people who, thanks to the intimacy they have developed with God, attract the favors of God not only in their life, but also in the people around them, without even them realizing it sometimes. Indeed, how many realize that if they are still alive, it is thanks to the prayers of a father, a mother, or a relative who would constantly stand before God in their favor?

The relationship between God and Moses was such that those who attacked Moses dealt directly with God. One day, Miriam and Aaron, Moses's brother and sister, talked against him, because they blamed him for the fact that his wife was Ethiopian. On hearing their criticisms, God summoned them both and told them:

> *"Listen to my words: when there is a prophet among you, I, the LORD, reveal myself to them in visions, I speak to them in dreams. But this is not true of my servant Moses; he is faithful in all my house.* **With him I speak face to face, clearly and not in riddles; he sees the form of the LORD.** *Why then were you not afraid to speak against my servant Moses?"*
> (Numbers 12:6-8)

After these words, Miriam was struck with white leprosy, but she was healed thanks to the intervention of Moses, who asked for the mercy of God. Nevertheless, she was forced to stay seven days outside the camp, the time for leprosy to vanish completely. This story is a good illustration of the fact that the close friends of God have a privileged relationship with Him. However, God is also very demanding towards those He let in his circle of close friends. The way Moses ended his life is significant. He was destined to lead the people until the promised land and finally he could not enter. Actually, one day, the people of Israel were once again complaining about having left Egypt to end up in the desert, because there was no water for them and for their herd. God asked Moses to summon him and to talk to the rock, from which He would make water come out. Moses did as he was told by the Eternal, but instead of simply talking to the rock, he struck with his stick and said to the people: *"Listen, you rebels, must we bring you water out of this rock?"* (Numbers 20:10). Moses was so dissatisfied with the behavior of his people that he indulged in anger. However, the Bible tells us that he was considered at the time as being the most patient man on Earth (Numbers 12:3). But because he had not obeyed God, he who was his representative before the people, Moses was severely punished. Finally, his faithful servant Joshua will bring the people into the Promised land in his place.

- **Enter a true intimacy with God**

God is accessible to every individual and this, evenly. However, what enables some people to come as close as possible to Him and to develop a true closeness, is the disposition of their heart. In his Sermon on the Mount, Jesus told the attending people: *"Blessed are <u>the pure in heart</u>, for they will see God"* (Matthew 5:8). The Parole Vivante version translates this verse this way: "Blessed are those who are sincere and righteous; for they will see God". **A sincere and upright heart is the key that can open the door of God's heart, and to see Him face to face.** The state of Man's heart is decisive to enter a true intimacy with God, because He keeps his intimacy for those whose dispositions of the heart are pleasant to him.

Intimacy is the highest level of relationship; it equates to the deep love that should exist between a husband and his wife. Even if the Bible says that: *"God does not show favoritism"* (Romans 2:11), it is obvious that those who managed to enter the sphere of his intimacy see another aspect of his personality to which others do not have access. They are entitled to his secrets, receive the revelation of some mysteries and are sometimes even informed of things to come.

Peter, John and James had a privileged relationship with Jesus, compared to the rest of the other disciples. When Jairus, the ruler of the synagogue, found Jesus because his daughter was dying, the only disciples that Jesus allowed to enter Jairus's house with Him were Peter, John and James (Luke 8:51). During his transfiguration on the mountain, Jesus only was with Peter, John and James (Luke 9:28). During a meal, Peter asked John who was leaning on the chest of Jesus, to ask Him who the traitor was among them. John asked Jesus the question and He answered that he was the one to whom He would give the loaf of bread (John 13:26), and Jesus gave it to Judas. Jesus revealed to John who was going to give Him up, even if apparently, he did not completely realize it, since there was no reaction from him, even after the treason of Judas. A short while before the cross, Jesus went to the garden of Gethsemane with his disciples, in order to talk with his Father. He asked them to sit, then He withdrew with Peter, John and James (Mark 14:32). Likewise, Jesus chose later John the Apostle to reveal to him the book of Revelations, and tell him things that will happen at the end of times (Revelation 1:1).

How to walk in a true intimacy with God?

The History of mankind begins with a marriage, Adam and Eve's. The marriage of a man and a woman is an image of the relationship that should exist between God and human beings. Based on that idea, I would like to give you two simple keys to help you develop a true closeness with the Creator.

- <u>**First key:**</u> **Focus your attention on God**

Adam and Eve used to be intimate with God, He would come and talk with them in the evening, when the bustle of the day would dwindle away. Learning seclusion with God is essential, far from the noise and lapse in concentration, as well as taking time to focus all of your attention on Him, to learn to know Him and to be provided with instructions for our life. It is also this way that we receive advice from God, that we remain under his gaze and that we know which way to give to our existence (Psalm 32:8)

- <u>**Second key:**</u> **Be true before God**

At the beginning, Adam and Eve were naked and did not see anything wrong with that. At that time, their heart was holy, with no ulterior motive whatsoever. It is only after having disobeyed that they were ashamed and tried to hide. The purity of their heart would suit God's presence, since He would come to visit them in the evening. So, a true and crystal-clear heart, that is to say naked before God, attracts His presence in our lives.

3 - Foregoing one's life to follow Christ

Jesus is *the image of the invisible God* (Colossians 1:15), *the radiance of God's glory and the exact representation of his being* (Hebrews 1:3). He is the only one who has been able to declare to the Father with certainty: *"I have brought you glory on Earth by finishing the work you gave me to do."* (John 17:4). If we too want to glorify God, we have a duty to discover what He wants us to achieve, by relying on the model of life of Jesus Christ. **The ultimate goal of every born-again believer should be to strive to be like Jesus Christ, to make Him visible on Earth, and this way, by seeing Him, people**

believe in Him and in God. Paul, the apostle, wrote to the inhabitants of Ephesus by inviting them to become imitators of Christ. He told them:

> *"**Follow God's example**, there-fore, as dearly loved children and walk in the way of love, just as Christ loved us and gave himself up for us as a fragrant offering and sacrifice to God. (Ephesians 5:1-2)"*

In order to reach this, it is essential to get closer to Jesus by letting the Holy Spirit turn us into his image, thus knowing Him in depth. By studying his life, we can draw principles and teachings that will enable us in our turn to impact the environment and the time in which we live. Our family, our friends, our workmates and society need to see Him to believe, for if most of the people do not believe in God, it is simply because they do not see Him. But if more people decide to give up on their lives and follow the steps of Jesus Christ, He will then become visible through them, and people around them will be able to see Him and to believe. Jesus has come to reveal the Father, but also to present a new life model accessible to every believer, as long as he accepts to give up on his life to follow Him wholeheartedly:

> *"Whoever wants to be my disciple must deny themselves and take up their cross and follow me. For whoever wants to save their life will lose it, but whoever loses their life for me will find it."* (Matthew 16:24-25)

In western society, the idea that it is necessary to forego one's life is a greatly misunderstood notion, because we have been taught from an early age that we control our existence:

"It is my life!", "I'm free!", "I do what I want to do!". Three sentences that most of us have already said or thought at least once in our teenage years. To understand this notion of giving up, we must begin with answering this question: Do I really control my life?

The people who choose to give up their life to follow Christ are those who have become aware that everything that led their existence was in conflict with the principles of God, and consequently would cause them harm. Perhaps they were not necessarily evil people, but their spirit having been lightened up by the revelation of God, they realize at present that they were prisoners of a way of thinking and a lifestyle, whereas they thought they were free. Wanting to free themselves from every sort of captivity, they voluntarily choose to walk away from what would keep them far from God, because the Holy Spirit has revealed to them the mystery that was hiding behind giving up on their life to follow Christ. Jesus Christ having come to set the captives free (Luke 4:19), they know they have access to freedom in Christ, from the moment they put their life under his authority. This can seem disconcerting for many of us, who have grown up in a culture in which we have been told that freedom consisted in acting as we please. It seems inconceivable for them that someone can claim to be free, whereas he gives the control of his life to God. This reaction is absolutely normal, because as long as they have not received the revelation of the love from God, they do not understand who He is, how much He loves them and what He has destined them for. By contrast, as soon as they have the revelation, the only thing they want is to put their lives in his hands too. For, by giving Him the first place, they inherit all the promises He has made for them.

ADVICE N°2

Adopt the qualities that please the heart of God

The human heart is the conductor of our organism. It relentlessly sends many orders to our different organs, which enables our body to function correctly. As for our spiritual heart, it is the core of our spiritual life. You can recognize a spiritually healthy heart from the peace and joy springing from it, whereas a heart in poor health is quite often prisoner of fear, anger and all kinds of negative feelings. The Bible advises us on several occasions to ensure to take care of our heart, as shows us the following verse: *"Above all else, guard your heart, for everything you do flows from it."* (Proverbs 4:23). Depending on the biblical passages, translators have chosen to use the word "heart" to describe the spirit or the soul, but in general, the "heart" usually corresponds to the spirit of Man.

One of the best ways to watch over our heart, to avoid any unpleasant surprise at the end of our race, is to develop a deep intimacy with the person of the Holy Spirit. In fact, one of his major roles is to lead us into all truth (John 16:13). For this purpose, He encourages us to meditate on the Bible regularly, because it enables us to judge our hearts, to examine our thoughts and our emotions, and this way to consider what is good and what is evil, what is true and what is not. Look at the powerful work the Word of God performs in our hearts:

*"For the word of God is alive and active. Sharper than any double-edged sword, it penetrates even to dividing soul and spirit, joints and marrow; **it judges <u>the thoughts</u> <u>and attitudes</u> <u>of the heart</u>.** Nothing in all creation is hidden from God's sight. **Everything is uncovered and laid bare before the eyes of him to whom we must give account."***
(Hebrews 4:12-13)

Verse 13: ***"Everything is uncovered and laid bare before the eyes of him to whom we must give account."***, is really interesting for it shows us that even if we have a certain outward attitude, our hearts are laid bare before God, and that He sees us as we really are. That is why God told through the mouth of prophet Jeremiah: *"I the LORD search the heart and examine the mind, to reward each person according to their conduct, according to what their deeds deserve."* (Jeremiah 17:10). King David, who was a man according to the heart of God, grasped the importance of constantly having a pure heart before God. When he would make a mistake, he would ask God for mercy, in order to preserve his relationship with Him unspoiled, which was more precious than anything else. After having committed adultery with Bathsheba, the wife of Uriah, he wrote a penitential Psalm in which he asks for forgiveness for his sin: *"Hide your face from my sins and blot out all my iniquity.* ***Create in me a pure heart****, O God, and renew a steadfast spirit within me. Do not cast me from your presence or take your Holy Spirit from me."* (Psalm 51:9-11). David had understood that the presence of the Holy Spirit at his side greatly depended on the state of his heart. Thus, keeping a pure and rightful heart before God should be our daily priority, because without that, we cannot develop a good relationship with God. But when our heart is pure before God, it is at that moment that his glory can truly manifest itself in our lives.

It reads in the Bible: *"All a person's ways seem pure to them, but motives are weighed by the LORD."* (Proverbs 16:2). It is easy to believe that we are in truth, as long as what we see and understand is in accordance with our convictions. But the only truly legitimate person to define what is true and what is wrong, is none other than God.

In this second part, I have chosen to deal with four essential qualities it is important to develop, because they are particularly pleasant to the heart of God and influence our environment. It deals with: love, obedience, humility and faithfulness. Needless to say that there are many others, which are as important, such as: the fear of the Lord, sanctification or forgiveness.

Chapter 1
Love

"My son, if your heart is wise,
then my heart will be glad indeed."
(Proverbs 23:15)

Modern society likes to portray the Creator as being an imaginary God, or a God remote from the concerns of men, some not even hesitating to credit Him with the responsibility for all the pains they suffer. This description is, of course, at odds with reality, since God is love, and Man is, on the contrary, at the center of all his attention. From Genesis to Revelation, the Bible tells us a love story between God and his Creation, although this story has constantly been jeopardized by Man's persisting disloyalty, who repeatedly turned away from Him to worship idols and foreign gods. One of the most remarkable events is certainly the one following the leaving of Egypt, when the people were getting impatient to see Moses who was late coming back, because he had withdrawn to talk with God. After having waited several days, they decided to make a golden calf and to worship it, whereas they had attended tremendous miracles, among which the split of the Red Sea in two. All along the Old Testament, we see God blessing the people of Israel, and how they end up turning away from Him after a while. It is important to notice that as long as they were loyal to God, blessings and protection rested on them. However, as soon as they turned away from Him to serve and worship other gods, He would grant them some time to come back to Him, but if they refused, they would be struck by devastation and Divine judgment. Is it not surprising that they turn away from the living God to turn to mere objects made of wood and metal? Let us look at a verse describing the way the Bible speaks about idols:

> *"But their idols are silver and gold, made by human hands. They have mouths, but cannot speak, eyes, but cannot see. They have ears, but cannot hear, noses, but cannot smell. They have hands, but cannot feel, feet, but cannot walk, nor can they utter a sound with their throats. Those who make them will be like them, and so will all who trust in them."* (Psalm 115:4- 8)

God is a jealous God, and his love to Man is exclusive. He refuses to share it with other gods, which are either demonic spiritual entities (evil spirits) or man-made objects (idols). That is the reason why He firmly recommended to Moses: *"Do not worship any other god, for the Lord, whose name is Jealous, is a jealous God."* (Exodus 34:14). We could think that this is outdated, but how many people keep having idols in their life? For some, it can be about sacred objects before which they bow down or wear as a talisman. For others, it can be their home, their very last car, their money, their professional career, or even someone who has the first place in their heart. Indeed, how many say they "adore" their child, their partner, their favorite singer or club? Feeling very strong love for a relative or someone we admire is normal, but adoration is normally restricted to God and to Him only (Luke 4:8). Some people will say it is just a way of speaking, not always realizing that they have raised these people on the same level as God in their heart. Let us always remember that *the mouth speaks what the heart is full of* (Luke 6:45). In other words, there is always some truth in what we can say, even if it is sometimes a joke.

God demands us to love Him thoroughly. He loves us with true love, like a husband loves his wife and cannot bear her desertion to love somebody else than him. His look is constantly directed to his beloved people, and whoever touches them, touches the apple of his eye (Zechariah 2:8). The people of Israel are in the image of the men and women who fill the Earth. Indeed, how often have we too turned away from God? How often have we let someone or something take the first place on the throne of our heart? In spite of our many failings, God remains faithful in his love and keeps blessing all men whoever they are. As Jesus said during the Sermon on the mount: *"He causes his sun to rise on the evil and the good, and sends rain on the righteous and the unrighteous"* (Matthew 5:45). But his commitment has certainly not come to an end here, since at the time He had set beforehand, God pushed his love to the utmost by giving his beloved Son in sacrifice for the salvation of mankind. The cross is considered as foolishness by those who cannot grasp the scope of it, for it is only through revelation that the power of this act can be understood (1 Corinthians 1:18). Only those who receive the meaning of the cross can realize how much they are precious in the eyes of their Creator.

1 - God is love

God is love. Three simple words, but so powerful to describe the infinite greatness of the love of God. These words were written by John the Apostle, nicknamed by some as "the apostle of love" because of the proximity he had with Jesus Christ and the revelation he had of the love of the Father. Let us have a look at what he wrote about love, under the inspiration of the Holy Spirit:

> *"Dear friends, let us love one another, for love comes from God. Everyone who loves has been born of God and knows God. Whoever does not love does not know God,* **because God is love.** *This is how God showed his love among us: He sent his one and only Son into the world that we might live through him. This is love: not that we loved God, but that he loved us and sent his Son as an atoning sacrifice for our sins. Dear friends, since God so loved us, we also ought to love one another. No one has ever seen God; but if we love one another, God lives in us and his love is made complete in us."* (1 John 4:7-12)

The Greek word used for "love" is *"agapè"*, which means **unconditional love**. God loves us unconditionally, and He cannot be otherwise, because this is what He is, He is love. When we need our love to be motivated by something to be able to manifest it, God, as to Him, loves everybody invariably, whatever the color of skin, the language or the social status.

Some will surely say: "If God is Love, why does the Bible mention the Last Judgment?" During the period of grace, God gives men and women free choice to accept or to refuse his love. Those who accept it and believe that He has manifested it through his only Son, make the choice of welcoming Jesus Christ in their life as their Lord and personal Savior. The Spirit of God then comes to put his love in them, as a seal proving his presence, as explains to us the following verse: "*And hope does not put us to shame, **because God's love has been poured out into our hearts through the Holy Spirit, who has been given to us.***" (Romans 5:5)

One day, a young adult related to me her testimony and the way she was convinced of the existence of God. She used to be an atheist, due to the fact that she had grown up with her mother who neither believed in God. One day, as she was alone in her apartment, she simply asked God to manifest Himself to her in a concrete way if He really existed. After having said these simple words, she felt the presence of God engulfing the room and the love of God overwhelming her. This love was so strong that she could not resist and burst into tears during several long minutes. While she was crying, a reconciliation took place in her, between her and her Creator. She received that day the certainty of the existence of God and his love for her. It is worth noticing that nobody intervened in this meeting, but that her quest for truth led her to the Creator. This testimony recalls the fact that God lets Himself be found by those who look for Him (Jeremiah 29:14).

At the beginning, Adam and Eve too had this unconditional love, but it was unfortunately corrupted by sin. From that day on, our love has become purely selective. As for now, we choose to love our family, our close friends, or the people with whom we have some physical attraction, affinities or common interests. Love is the shared foundation on which all mankind rests, and if it had to completely disappear one day, it would only entail the absolute destruction of society. **Human beings need to love and to feel loved to exist and to be fully alive.** The degradation of family relationships, the prevailing atmosphere of mistrust in some great metropolises, the incivilities and acts of violence daily reported in the crime section, have no other reason than the dissolution of this love. But is it that surprising after all, in a growingly individualistic world? Jesus warned his disciples that in the last days, *because of the increase of wickedness, the love of most will grow cold* (Matthew 24:12). God's love is the only ingredient able to reconcile men and women between them, and with Him. Any person willing to be filled with this love must come and quench his thirst from the Spring which is nothing else than God Himself.

2 - The royal law of love

After four hundred and thirty years of slavery in Egypt, God gave different commandments to the people of Israel, so that they free themselves from bad customs they had adopted during their servitude, and readjust their thoughts on his, to behave and think as a free people from this moment on. According to the rabbinic tradition, the Jewish law is made of six hundred and thirteen commandments. You may as well say that, very few people know them as a whole, and even fewer are able to respect them in their entirety. The requirements are such that sinning against one of these commandments amounts to sinning against all the law (James 2:10). However, the whole of these laws can be summed up in only one commandment: *"Love your neighbor as yourself."* (Romans 13:9). The Bible calls this prescription the royal law, as we can see in this verse: *"If you really keep the royal law found in Scripture, "Love your neighbor as yourself," you are doing right."* (James 2:8). Jesus is the only one who managed to completely obey the laws as a whole, because no sin has been found in Him. The man and the woman who decide to love the other like themselves, refuse to harm him, and by acting this way, accomplish in some way all the law. The laws of a state are used to protect us and to protect others, but if everyone decides to do well, they finally become useless. If everyone chooses love instead of evil, violence and crime will no longer exist, and society will then be deeply transformed. Of course, it is not about any love, but more precisely about love *agapè*, that is to say unconditional love that does not care about appearances and does not aim at one's own interests, but looks rather for the others' above all. The cultural criteria that usually make us appreciate a person, depending on what we like, finally have no place. For the more someone is filled with the love of God, the more the look he takes at the others changes, because he now sees them as God sees them. Likewise, the people surrounding him can feel the love of God which strongly emanates through him. God's will is to spread his love over the Earth, and this through his children. Love should be the sign that a man or a woman belongs to God. Unfortunately, this is not always the case, sometimes it is even quite the contrary by the way. What can be the reason for that? God's love has not managed to penetrate the hearts.

3 - Love: the only prerogative to please God

One day, the disciples asked Jesus to teach them how to pray. He taught them how to pray, by starting with the two following verses: *"Our Father in heaven, hallowed be your name, **your kingdom come**, your will be done, on earth as it is in heaven."* (Matthew 6:9-10). I would especially like to draw your attention to the following sentence: *"**your kingdom** *come"*. **God has a kingdom for which he has established his son Jesus Christ as being the King.** Every kingdom is governed by laws, and the kingdom of God's main law is none other than love. God has sent his Son on the Earth out of love, Jesus gave his life out of love, and the Holy Spirit has chosen to dwell in the born-again believers, so that they will not be alone. Love is the foundation of the Kingdom of God, and every born-again Christian should be recognized by the love he manifests around him. Our love being imperfect, the Holy Spirit has come to pour out the perfect love of God in us. This love enables us to love *Him*, to love the others, but also ourselves, because many do not love themselves. The presence of the Holy Spirit should be made visible through our attitude, by what the Bible calls: the fruit of the Spirit. The fruit of the Spirit is nothing else than the character of Christ. Paul, the apostle introduces it in the book of Galatians: *"But the fruit of the Spirit is **<u>love</u>, joy, peace, forbearance, kindness, goodness, faithfulness, gentleness and self-control.**"* (Galatians 5:22-23). You will have noticed that among these nine characteristics, the very first attribute presented by Paul is love. The fact that he has chosen to quote it first is no coincidence, because if we have a close look at each one of them, we can see that they all come from love. Imagine for example a tree; the trunk and its roots represent love and its branches the virtues originating from this love. Let us have a look together, with the Word to back it up.

- **Joy**: *"Then make my joy complete by being like-minded, **having the same love,** **being one in spirit and of one mind.**"* (Philippians 2:2)

- **Peace:** *"There is no fear in love. **But perfect love drives out fear**, because fear has to do with punishment. The one who fears is not made perfect in love."* (1 John 4:18)

- **Patience**: "*Be completely humble and gentle; be patient, **bearing with one another in love.***" (Ephesians 4:2)

- **Kindness**: "*The LORD appeared to us in the past, saying: **I have loved you with an everlasting love; I have drawn you with unfailing kindness.***" (Jeremiah 31:3)

- **Goodness**: "***Be devoted to one another in love.** Honor one another above yourselves.*" (Romans 12:10)

- **Faithfulness**: "*Though the mountains be shaken and the hills be removed, yet **my unfailing love for you will not be shaken** nor my covenant of peace be removed, says the LORD, who has compassion on you.*" (Isaiah 54:10)

- **Gentleness**: "*I urge you to live a life worthy of the calling you have received. Be completely humble and gentle; be patient, **bearing with one another in love.***" (Ephesians 4:1-2)

- **Temperance** (self-control): "*For the Spirit God gave us does not make us timid, but **gives us power, love and self-discipline**.*" (2 Timothy 1:7)

- **Ensuring not to allow the works of God take his place**

Just before going up to Heaven, Jesus recommended that his disciples stay in Jerusalem until they receive the power from above, that is to say the Holy Spirit. Every born-again Christian must yearn for the baptism of the Holy Spirit, for it bestows on him the gifts and power he needs to fully manifest the Kingdom of God on the Earth, thus making Christ visible to our contemporaries. However, it is important to keep watch over one's heart, so as not to get carried away by activism. In fact, it is important to make a clear distinction between, on the one hand, our relationship with God, and, on the other hand, our actions contributing to the progress of his work. Many Christians commit themselves body and soul to their service for God, and devote a huge amount of time for it, often at the expense of their relationship and their intimacy with Him. They do not necessarily see any problem with it, because they are convinced that their work is proof of their love for God. They are so absorbed by all kinds of activities that they do not even think about taking some time to sit down and think. They keep going this way, unawares of the fact that over time, God is no longer by their side. Their works have taken the first place onto the throne of their heart, and have stealthily ejected God from his seat. A quiet coup d'état has taken place in their heart, in which the King has been replaced by another king: works.

It will not be long before this change of power brings a spiritual cooling, even if many do not notice it straight away. Because they are convinced that God is still with them, due to the fact that they keep manifesting gifts. The people who are attentive to the Holy Spirit will soon realize it and put things right, but others may draw away from God without even noticing it, even though they keep manifesting signs and miracles. Someone whose way of thinking has not been renewed can easily be caught up in congratulation, solicitudes and fame flattering his ego. This sort of person wallows in an acknowledgement and a self-esteem highlighted by the fact that he attracts looks on him instead of God. Watching over one's heart is important, since it is very easy to get carried away. That is the reason why God can allow us to go through a period of "breaking", to bring to highlight the flaws of our character such as vanity, jealousy, criticism, complaint or a lack of love.

Actually, if they are not treated early enough, they can become an occasion of fall much later. How many have had a good start before success or activities draw them away from God? Some people even confess having lost their first love, and thank God for having taken them back at the right moment, since they know that they would have been very unpleasantly surprised once they would find themselves before Him.

In April 2016, I attended a prophetic conference in the city of Lancaster, in the United States. One of the participants, a world-famous prophet who would travel everywhere in the world to serve God, acknowledged that at one time in his ministry, he had totally lost his first love for God. He was so engrossed in the service that his love for God had little by little dwindled away, without him even realizing it. He explained how much love is fundamental, particularly in the prophetic ministry, because a prophet or a prophetess is a canal through which God liberates his word. Yet, a man and a woman of God who lack love can corrupt the message they have to deliver, by judging and hurting the person to whom they speak. God being love, somebody who speaks in his Name must manifest love in the message he delivers, except, of course, if the Holy Spirit has expressly asked him to do otherwise. He illustrated his arguments by giving the testimony of Bob Jones, another world-famous prophet who had lived a supernatural experience. As he was dying, he was caught up to the third heaven and saw Jesus face to face. He explained that the only question Jesus asked him when he found himself opposite Him was: "Did you learn how to love?" When he realized that he had not known how to love, Jesus sent him back on the Earth[1]. Suddenly, he woke up from the coma, and understood that day

---

1. Testimony of Bob Jones, "Bob Jones died- God sent him back from heaven's": https://www.youtube.com/watch?v=3MRJ3wA5neU.

that, even though he was well known from men, he had to be known from God above all, and that the only way was to love the others as He does.

Making a clear distinction between our works and what motivates them is crucial. Love is the only prerogative to be pleasant to God, and our actions will be judged depending on the intentions of our heart, whether they are animated by love or by our personal interest. Once again, God is not impressed by the greatness of our actions, the size of our ministry, the number of our works, nor even by our title in the Church. God is mostly interested in the state of our heart and our ability to demonstrate his love, because our contemporaries will see this way that we are from Him. Jesus Himself warned us about not being mistaken about our aim. He said about this topic:

> *"Not everyone who says to me, 'Lord, Lord,' will enter the kingdom of heaven, but only the one who does the will of my Father who is in heaven. Many will say to me on that day, 'Lord, Lord, did we not prophesy in your name and in your name drive out demons and in your name perform many miracles?' Then I will tell them plainly, **'I never knew you**. Away from me, you evil-doers!'"* (Matthew 7:21-23)

I would particularly draw your attention to the sentence: **"I never knew you"**. Each time this expression is used in the Bible, it is usually for describing the intimacy existing between two spouses, that is to say the sexual act. Here are a few examples:

*"And Adam **knew** Eve his wife;
and she conceived, and bare Cain,
and said, I have gotten a man from
the LORD."* (Genesis 4:1)

*"And Cain **knew** his wife; and
she conceived, and bare Enoch:
and he builded a city, and called
the name of the city, after the name
of his son, Enoch."* (Genesis 4:17)

*"Elkanah **knew** Hannah his
wife; and the LORD remembered
her."* (1 Samuel 1:19)

Jesus deliberately chooses to use this expression: **"I never knew you"**, to point out that He has no relationship, no intimacy with those people. This passage has always made me stop and caught my attention, because I have always wondered how people who clearly manifest the power of God could finally be disqualified, for it is mainly what this is about. The Bible teaches us that God's gifts and his call are irrevocable (Romans 11:29). Consequently, a person may very well have started with God and have been sincere in his commitment, and unfortunately move away from Him, even though gifts keep working. That is the reason why Jesus emphasizes the fact that the tree is known by its fruits. Someone filled with the Holy Spirit will manifest the fruit of the Spirit, whereas someone who has gone astray from God will very difficultly conceal his true character. Some people make it for a while, but only a particular event is enough for the mask to fall, and for their true content to be exposed to the light of day. No matter how filled their mouth is with nice sentences and sometimes even nice verses, their behavior is totally out of step with manifesting the character of Christ. They admittedly bear fruit, but it is covered with thorns and has a very bitter taste, especially for their entourage. Conversely, a man and a woman whose heart is radiated by the love of God, relay the life of God around them, each time they communicate.

4 - The perfect love of God

In his first letter to the Corinthians, Paul, the apostle presents the different spiritual gifts and explains their use in chapters twelve and fourteen. He concludes chapter 12 with this last sentence: *"Now eagerly desire the greater gifts. **And yet I will show you the most excellent way.**" (*1 Corinthians 12:31). This verse brings in chapter 13, by preparing the believers of Corinth to receive a revelation surpassing everything he taught them before. In chapter 13, he solely addresses the subject of love and the definition he gives is simply outstanding. Why has Paul made the choice of talking about love in the midst of his description of spiritual gifts? He wanted to demonstrate that spiritual gifts are absolutely worthless without love. **Love is the multiplying factor which determines the true worth of our acts in the eyes of God, and without love, all our actions equal to zero.** Love is the divine substance giving supernatural dimensions to gestures as simple as a smile, a handshake, a hug or a little help. God being love, the more someone spends time in his presence, the more his glory can but shine through him. This person fascinates and attracts people around him, because of the love he carries and which changes the environment in which he is.

Let us look at the definition of love as it is presented in 1 Corinthians 13, and the requirements demanded for everyone willing to manifest it.

"If I speak in the tongues of men or of angels, but do not have love, I am only a resounding gong or a clanging cymbal. If I have the gift of prophecy and can fathom all mysteries and all knowledge, and if I have a faith that can move mountains, but do not have love, I am nothing. If I give all I possess to the poor and give over my body to hardship that I may boast, but do not have love, I gain nothing.

Love is patient, love is kind. It does not envy, it does not boast, it is not proud. It does not dishonor others, it is not self-seeking, it is not easily angered, it keeps no record of wrongs. Love does not delight in evil but rejoices with the truth. It always protects, always trusts, always hopes, always perseveres. Love never fails. *But where there are prophecies, they will cease; where there are tongues, they will be stilled; where there is knowledge, it will pass away."*
(1 Corinthians 13:1-8)

This definition cannot leave anybody indifferent, since the standards are so high. It addresses us all, believers as non-believers, because it encourages us to question ourselves on our own love. Love as it is presented in this passage goes way beyond the love that can exist between a man and a woman, or between a parent and his child. It is an absolute and endless love that God wishes to pour out in every individual, so that human beings realize how much He loves them. It is the same love that Jesus Christ manifested on Earth, and this until the cross. As He was nailed to wood, suspended between the sky and the Earth, and people were insulting and provoking Him by asking Him to free Himself if He really was the Son of God, He kept remaining in love against all odds, asking his Father to forgive them because they did not know what they were doing (Luke 23:24). This love is supernatural, it goes over every human understanding, it is the love of God. Every born-again person receives this love when the Holy Spirit comes to dwell in him, and everybody's role not only consists in maintaining it, but also in developing it in order to fully manifest it around. The love of God is powerful enough to restore the soul, heal the broken hearts, change the character and bring life back to everything that was dead in us.

Chapter 2
Obedience

"Whoever does God's will is
my brother and sister and mother."
(Mark 3:35)

One of the most wanted characteristics in a man and a woman of God is obedience. The word obedience is very often misunderstood, particularly by a number of people who see it more as a constraint than as something possibly beneficial for them. However, everybody will acknowledge that for community life to be possible, it is necessary that citizens obey the laws of the country in which they live, as well as their duties. This way, obedience to these rules enables every one of us to live freely, and also to be in harmony with one another. So where does this wrong conception come from? For some, it goes back to our teenage years, when we were forced to obey our parents, a teacher or an adult, even if we did not necessarily feel like doing so. In the midst of the discovery of the world around us, instructions such as: "Be careful!", "Don't do that!", "Don't touch!", "Stand up straight!", "Look ahead!", "Tidy your room!", have enabled us to have a well-defined setting and this way to set our limits. If at the time we considered them as *impediments to our freedom*, they have turned out over time to be as foundations on which we have relied to grow up and become the people we are today. A man said one day: "I regret that my parents were way too lenient with me, because if they had been a little stricter, it would have saved me from making many mistakes." He acknowledged that the absence of setting and limits has caused him a lot of trouble at an adult age. Some will say that it is through life experiences that we learn to become oneself, and that is true. But others will say that a better setting during their childhood would have enabled them to make fewer mistakes and harm around them.

So what is exactly obedience? Obedience consists in submitting to the will of someone, respecting a law or rules. As orders always come from someone or some entity, the most important is not so much the obligation requirement in itself, but rather the person or the group that gives it to us, whether its intentions meant to us are good or bad. **The worth of an order or a law depends on the person or the entity at the origin of it, whether their personal interest is primarily sought or ours**. Thus, our obedience is based on two things: the first element is the one who gives the order and the second one is the order in itself. The first depends on how much we trust the person or the entity asking us to obey, and the second is directly linked to the intentions of the one who gives us the order.

I am sure you will admit that it is a lot easier to obey someone whom we know well that he has good intentions towards us, and that the contrary is more complicated for us. As long as this mutual trust is not entrenched, obeying remains something very difficult, for children as well as for adults, because human beings do not like submission. When trust is established, obeying is merely a detail at last, because even if it can cost us dear, we know that the intentions regarding us are benevolent. **Obedience is then no longer seen as a mere act,**

but also as the involvement of the heart, which encourages us to want to please the other. The obedient person no longer feels prejudiced or inferior, because a win-win relationship then takes place.

On the spiritual level, obedience is the bridge between God and man. It is the entry point enabling to establish a genuine relationship with him. Obedience to God is one of, if not THE essential prerequisite for a real relationship to be established between Him and the human beings. It is of such an important character to Him that as little as a single mistake from Adam and Eve was needed to end the intimacy they had woven. This decision might seem harsh at first glance, but it is important to underline that by disobeying God, Adam and Eve preferred following their own will rather than God's. Their deed implies that they estimated their will better than his, and it is precisely on this point that they committed a mistake. Indeed, their transgression did not only lie in the violation of the divine order, but rather in the questioning of his Author's will, who only wished them good. Any person convinced that his will is better than God's is unfortunately wrong, because just as parents want what is best for their child, God also wishes the best for every human being. By rejecting his order, Adam and Eve accepted to believe that He could have lied to them, and thus tried to treat them unfairly. From that day on, the heart of Man has been totally corrupted by sin.

Obedience to God is in no way a deprivation of freedom as many believe, but it is actually the way of touching his heart and thus to enjoy his love, his peace, his joy and his many other blessings. Anyone who understands that will naturally tend to obey God, for he knows that He wants what is best for his life. Let us have a look at five advantages obedience to God provides us.

1 - Our obedience gives glory to God

God is utterly unimpressed by somebody's talent, because He is the Giver. No more is He impressed by his accomplishments, as important as they are, because they finally are but the materialization of an idea or a dream made possible thanks to the talent that He has Himself given. People who are successful in life have simply discovered the talent that God has given to them and have endeavored to develop it. It does not question the fact that they had to work hard to reach that goal, or for some of them to go over quite a number of hardships, but it is important to always keep in mind that God gives ability to men. This awareness must bring us to wonder about the use of our gifts and our talents. What do we do with them? Do we use them to make his will or ours? Paul, the apostle, wrote: *"For who makes you different from anyone else? What do you have that you did not receive? And if you did receive it, why do you boast as though you did not?"* (1 Corinthians 4:7). Whereas some brothers and sisters from the church of Corinth claimed themselves to be disciples of Paul the apostle and others of Apollos, Paul reminded them that they were both merely simple workers of God, servants of the mysteries and gifts that God had entrusted to them. Although Corinthians had been blessed through their intervention, they did not have to forget that all the glory had to be given back to God, and not to Paul and Apollos. This reminder enables us to always keep in mind that *every good and perfect gift is from above* (James 1:17). The important element that has to be taken into account is consequently the way we use the talent that has been entrusted to us. Somebody whose first concern is to please God will do his utmost to know His will. Once he has discovered it, he will look for the way to accomplish it, by setting his talent going and by associating the Holy Spirit, of course, because no work coming from God can be made without his involvement.

Most of the people are only interested in completed actions, that is to say what is visible, but God cannot be satisfied with that only. He looks into the heart of Man, to probe it and to know what really animates him. Testing the feelings of the heart enables Him to determine the genuine worth of a deed, because for an accomplishment to have a real importance to his eyes, it must be motivated by love before anything else. Love towards Him first, then love towards the other, our personal considerations only arriving third. Above all, we should not think that we lose out by putting aside our personal interests after the others', for having accomplished the will of God and looking upon the benefits in the life of the others make us truly satisfied.

Like salt makes food tasty, love is the essential ingredient for our actions to have a scope both in the natural world and in the spiritual world. When we grasp this, our way of acting changes and our wish is to align our will, our talents and our heart on his will, which gradually draws us closer to his perfection. This revelation provokes in us a strong feeling of humbleness, because we realize that God does neither look at the "greatness" of our actions (whose appreciation is most of the time subjective), nor the financial costs, or even the work required. Above all, God is interested in the motivations of our heart, for everything He asks us is quite often a way to test our obedience and, through that, to transform us little by little in his image.

2 - Our obedience assures us to walk in the plans of God

God has plans for every human being. As a good father, He wants the best for each of us, as shows us so well in this verse: "*For I know the plans I have for you, declares the LORD, plans to prosper you and not to harm you, plans to give you hope and a future.*" (Jeremiah 29:11). Obeying his will insures us to walk in the plans He has prepared beforehand for every one of us and to enjoy this way his many blessings. God knows the end of our story even before we started writing it. Obedience enables us to take the path He has set for us and move forward step by step. This does not mean that our life will be a long quiet river, but we must be confident that hardships and/or events through which we will go are under control. In fact, the Bible declares the following thing: "*And we know that in all things God works for the good of those who love Him, who have been called according to his purpose.*" (Romans 8:28). Having a clear understanding of the meaning of this verse is important, otherwise we may make the mistake of doing everything that crosses our minds, and of believing that God will settle all the situations in our favor. It is definitely written: "*all things God works for the good **of those who love Him***". The interesting question to eventually ask is: how do we recognize someone who truly loves God? The answer is given by Jesus Himself in the book of John when He tells his disciples: "***Whoever has my commands and keeps them is the one who loves me.** The one who loves me will be loved by my Father, and I too will love them and show myself to them.*" (John 14:21). In other terms, if I rephrase: "***Whoever knows my will and submits to it is the one who loves me***". We can see through those two verses that not only is our obedience evidence of our love towards Him, but it also insures us that whatever life situations we may face, they will end up turning to our advantage.

In 2016, I was in Los Angeles with Pascal, a friend, to attend *Azusa Now*, a great rally at Memorial Coliseum. Sixty thousand people had gathered to celebrate the anniversary of the one hundred and ten years of Azusa Street revival, which occurred in 1906 in Los Angeles. After the event, we had to go to Philadelphia for a conference. On arriving at the airport, we were unpleasantly surprised to learn that our flight was canceled and postponed to the day after. As I was complaining, Pascal simply told me: "*All things God works for the good of those who love Him. God is good!*" I must confess that at that moment, I did not really want to hear this kind of sentence. A woman who was behind us started smiling when she heard: "God is good!". She immediately started the conversation. She and her husband were a couple of ministers, and they had been invited to the event Azusa Now. We quickly gave each other our contact details to take time to talk after having checked in our luggage. When it was our turn, the operator told us that our flight was canceled and that the only available flights would leave the day after. I told him that we had to get a rental car at the Philadelphia airport that very evening and that at the hotel was also booked. He answered us: "I fully understand, give me just a moment". He stood up and went to another airline booth. He came back a few minutes later and told us that he had found available seats on the flight of another company. The tickets cost $1,500, but their company would pay for all the cost. The new tickets were a lot more advantageous than the former ones, because it was a direct flight, whereas there was a stopover in Dallas for our initial flight. That day, I was once again confirmed that indeed, all things God works for the good of those who love Him, because the flight cancelation turned to our favor. But this did not stop at that point. One year later, the pastoral couple we had met at the airport went into contact with my friend Pascal, who would live since then in the United States, to ask him if he had contacts in France, because a young girl from their church was on a trip in France. She just left for a few days, but when she arrived, God would have asked her to stay longer. The problem was that she knew nobody. Pascal gave them the address of the church and called a few people. She came to church on a Sunday morning and was moved by the welcome and the love she received. Several people got organized to accommodate her each one his turn. She stayed three months in France and before going back to the United States, she told us: "Now I understand why God wanted me to be here!". Her stay and the different meetings had deeply transformed her. She had received the love she needed to be spiritually and emotionally restored, and the teachings she had received had enlightened her concerning the call of God for her life. All of that started from a simple canceled flight. That is why when something unexpected happens, let us avoid complaining immediately, but let us wait to see the way God will step in, because *"All things God works for the good of those who love Him"*.

3 - Our obedience testifies that we belong to God

The Bible tells us this: *"You were bought at a price. Therefore honor God with your bodies."* (1 Corinthians 6:20). Every believer who has sincerely given his life to Christ knows that he does no longer belong to himself, but to God. From then on, his role consists in praising God, by discovering and accomplishing the goal for which he has been created. Obedience insures him to do what God expects from him and to become the person he has to be. It is important to keep in mind at all times that when society looks at *what we do* and *what we have*, God is, as for Him, focused on *what we are*. Modern society has created a sort of "virtuous circle" in which the human being is at the center, and everything must gravitate around him. This way of thinking implies that everything he undertakes must be directed towards him and the satisfaction of his needs. This is the reason why many imagine that their personal success goes through the fulfilment of their SELF: **my** delight, **my** interests, **my** money, **my** car, **my** house, **my** holidays, **my** children.

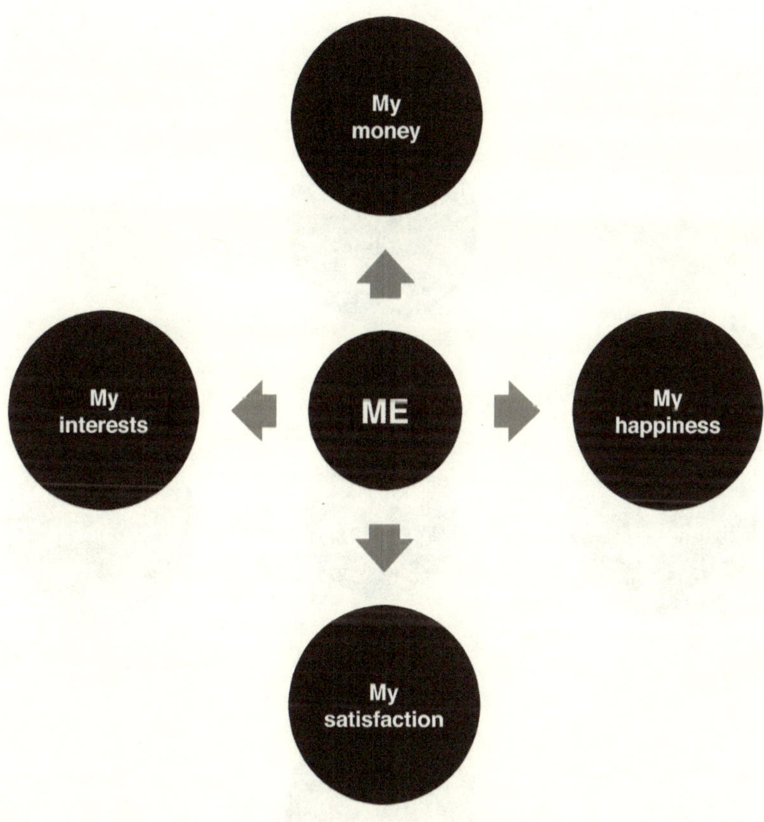

Anybody who thinks this way unavoidably meets hardships to submit to God, since obedience gives him the feeling of getting away from what can be good for him. Obeying God necessarily decentralizes the SELF, because God becomes the center and the Spring of <u>my</u> happiness, <u>my</u> satisfaction, <u>my</u> money, <u>my</u> car, <u>my</u> house, and <u>my</u> job. **In the same way the Earth moves around the sun and benefits from its light, God lights up everybody placing Him at the center of life, by becoming his Source and his Purveyor in all things.** Obedience gives us free access to what He has kept aside for each of us, and compels us not to rely on our own forces, but on Him and Him only.

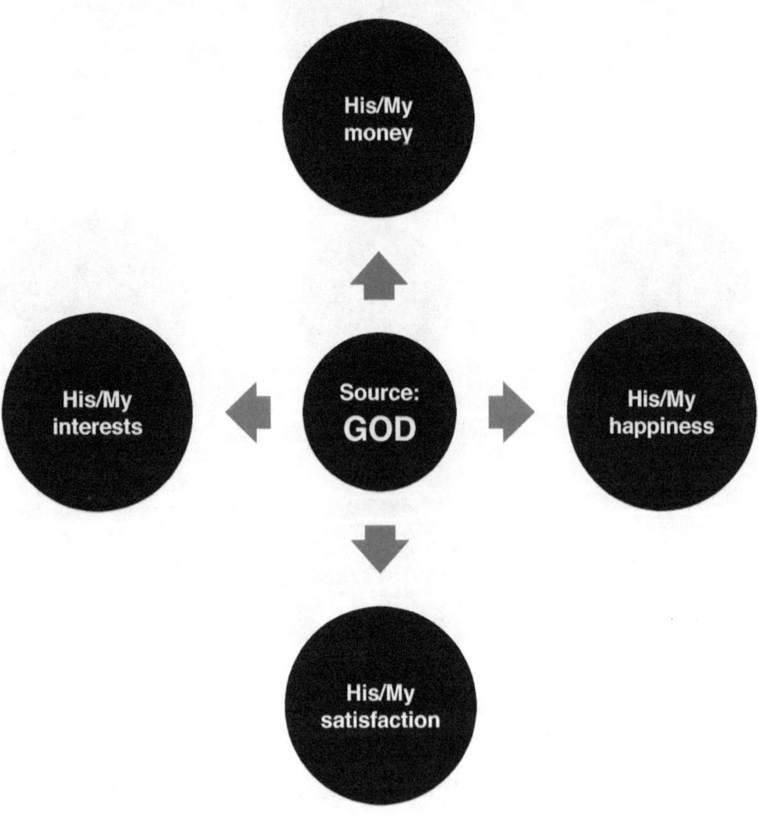

4 - Our obedience enables us to enter the supernatural

Jesus has left a promise for those who decide to take their cross and to follow him. He has told them: *"Very truly I tell you, whoever believes in me will do the works I have been doing, and they will do even greater things than these, because I am going to the Father."* (John 14:12). Throughout his earthly ministry, Jesus manifested the power of the Kingdom of God by driving out demons, healing the sick, raising the dead and teaching with authority. However, when we look around us, very few believers manage to really manifest the dimension of power in which God expects them. Obedience to the Word of God is one of the keys that enable miraculous things to happen, and the impossible to become possible. Just as an apprentice cook knows it is important if he wants his dish to turn out well, to follow the instructions of the chef carefully, the same is true for every born-again Christian who wishes to see the Heaven come down on Earth. He must read the Word of God, study it, meditate on it, memorize its key verses and most of all, believe it so as to put it into practice. Without faith, pleasing God is impossible (Hebrew 11:6). However, having faith in God and in his Word can give life to things that did not exist.

The more we take time to study the Bible, the more the Holy Spirit unveils the mysteries it contains. The Word of God is alive, and thanks to the lighting of the Holy Spirit, every reader who regularly looks into it finds a word of life producing in him encouragement, a confirmation or an idea in relationship with such and such a given situation. It is so precious that God said to Joseph, the successor of Moses: *"Keep this Book of the Law always on your lips; meditate on it day and night, so that you may be careful to do everything written in it. Then you will be prosperous and successful."* (Joshua 1:8). Obedience to the Word of God will bring success in every field of your life.

5 - Our obedience enables to identify adversity on a spiritual level

We will see in the third part that two worlds exist: the visible world and the invisible world, and that just as the physical world is governed by laws, the spiritual world is as well. The Word of God being Spirit and life (John 6:63), the instructions and recommendations It gives us have a scope both in the physical and in the spiritual world. Obeying the will of God, by submitting to his Word, protects us from the attacks of the adversary. Ignoring his principles and transgressing them can unfortunately expose us to danger, or even in some cases to death. I would like to share with you a true story, for you to understand that our ignorance can unfortunately cause our own downfall.

Bernard was a neighbor. His wife passed away and he had her cremated. He had put the ashes into a vase he had put on the edge of his fireplace. Every evening, he would talk to "his wife", tell her his day and how much he missed her. He told me one day: "Pascal, you will think that I'm crazy, but I talk to my wife and she visits me at night in my room when I sleep. She is so real that when she touches my arm, I can feel her hand on my skin". I answered him that I believed him, but he had to stop because he had got into contact with an evil spirit. Of course, he would not believe me. He was an atheist and believed in nothing. How surprising are people sometimes! He did not believe in God, but he believed that his wife came to visit him at night. He was himself aware that another world existed, but he refused to believe in God. Bernard practiced spiritism without even knowing it. Instead of talking to his wife, he had been in contact with a demonic spirit. Bernard struggled for several years against different cancers, and the most stunning thing is that whenever he seemed to be better, a new cancer would appear. He had opened a spiritual door without even knowing it and death would follow him relentlessly.

Chapter 3
Humbleness

"Humility is the fear of the LORD; its wages are riches and honor and life." (Proverbs 22:4)

One day, the disciples asked Jesus who will be the greatest among them in the Kingdom of Heaven. Jesus took a little child, placed him in the midst of them and told them: *"Therefore, whoever takes the lowly position of this child is the greatest in the kingdom of heaven."* (Matthew 18:4). By using this little child as an example, Jesus took them aback by completely upsetting their way of thinking. He chose this very young boy, who was not well considered in the eyes of the adults of the time, to teach them a secret of the Kingdom: **the greatness of someone is judged on his level of humbleness**. He wanted to show them through this example that the person who is humble-hearted will be elevated in heaven.

This story is interesting, because once again it shows us the huge discrepancy between the way of thinking of our western society and the Kingdom of God's. Going far to notice that is useless, you just have to switch on your television, to go on social networks or on video-sharing platforms such as

YouTube to see that people with the biggest number of fans are not necessarily always the humblest. Paradoxically, the more they put themselves first and pretend to be the best, the strongest, the nicest, and the more they are popular, or at least among the youngest who would also like to know the same glory.

The Cambridge dictionary defines humbleness as being: "The good quality of not being proud or not believing that you are important.[1]" Several passages of the Bible emphasize the necessity of being humble to be like Jesus. The Son of God, who has been from all time with the Father, voluntarily took off his glory and his magnificence to become a man. He made himself a servant by coming not to be served but to serve (Matthew 20:28), not to judge but to save. The Bible tells us that He lowered Himself until death:

> *"In your relationships with one another, have the same mindset as Christ Jesus: Who, being in very nature God, did not consider equality with God something to be used to his own advantage; rather,* **he made himself nothing by taking the very nature of a servant, being made in human likeness.** *And being found in appearance as a man,* **he humbled himself by becoming obedient to death** *— even death on a cross!"* (Philippians 2:5-8).

---

1. Cambridge Dictionary, website: https://dictionary.cambridge.org/dictionary/english/humbleness

He has accomplished things that no one had ever accomplished before Him and even after Him, and yet He has remained humble by systematically giving back the glory to God, because He knew that everything He would do was only possible thanks to his complete submission to the Father. Humbleness is an essential virtue to really please God, it is the key opening the doors of Heaven and enabling us to enjoy the numerous blessings of the Creator. Humbleness is a sign of greatness and a token of maturity in the Kingdom of God. It is a quality every born-again believer must manifest, because by showing humbleness, he acknowledges that everything he has or he is, does not depend on him after all, but on the grace of God. The handsome man, the clever woman, the athlete with outstanding abilities, the singer with an extremely nice voice, the scientist who discovers a vaccine, or the fashion creator who makes exceptional products, must recognize that God has created them this way, and He has given them creativity, intelligence, beauty, gifts and talents. Anybody aware of that tends to remain humble and grateful, by giving all the glory to the Creator. Let us look together at three points explaining why humbleness is so important in the eyes of God.

1 - Pride precedes destruction

A pastor who converted more than 45 years ago said one day to a young man who was congratulating him for his durability in the ministry: "I have noticed that three things bring down a man: women, money and pride". Pride is neither something to be taken lightly, nor to be considered as "a little fault", but on the contrary, it has to be tackled from the root before it takes up control. Pride is an exaggerated esteem of oneself, which makes us believe that we are superior to others. Pride is at the origin of many evils such as jealousy, criticism, mockery, arrogance or self-sufficiency. Nobody is immune to this plague which stealthily takes place in the hearts. Sometimes we are not even aware of its presence until a particular event enables it to come up. Some manage to hide it under a false appearance of humbleness, but some others cannot contain it and let it appear in broad daylight. They have a haughty look, talk with contempt and think they are superior, because they have the impression of being someone important. Physical beauty, intelligence, success, a professional promotion, a graduation, a sports victory, a challenge taken up, a social position reached, the purchase of a nice house or a nice car, fame, public acclaim, a photo or a video which receives many "likes", congratulations, acknowledgement and talent… These are the elements that feed the ego and swell the pride of those who have not taken care of treating it. All these things are not bad per se, but it is rather the effect they have on us that is either positive or negative, depending on the state of our heart. Pride misrepresents our vision of reality, and gives us the impression to be above the others and the center of everything.

People who had a good "start", but lost everything one day, are countless: an associate, a friend, their partner, their reputation, their money, their company or their position, because of the pride that invaded their heart. Disconnected from reality, they have hurt with their words, despised with their attitude, belittled a close friend or made a wrong choice. The story of Lucifer is significant in this respect. He used to be a cherub serving God, until the day when his heart swelled up because of his outstanding beauty. His pride was at the root of his fall (Ezekiel 28).

Pride has such a power over the human being, that the Bible warns us about this topic: *"Pride goes before destruction, a haughty spirit before a fall."* (Proverbs 16:18). It is important to watch over one's heart and to reject every form of pride to protect oneself. Those who are close to God will automatically be corrected by the Holy Spirit, who will unveil to them the state of their heart. Simply asking forgiveness to God and imploring his grace is enough to wipe out pride. Those who still move on according to the flesh will not necessarily realize it at once. There will have to be unfortunately an incident, or a remark from a relative to realize it. Those who question themselves will take into account the reproach that has been made to them, and will correct their attitude after introspection. By contrast, those who will not do this exercise will pretend to be the victim, which will obviously only increase their pride. It has to be understood that pride misrepresents our vision of reality, hence the importance of being sensitive to the voice of the Holy Spirit, or being surrounded with sincere friends, able to talk the truth, not to condemn us, but to help us correct ourselves and become a better person.

2 - Humbleness gives access to the throne of God

The quality of our prayers depends neither on their length nor on the variety of our vocabulary, but on their source, whether they are inspired by our flesh or by the Holy Spirit. John the apostle, who was taken up to the third heaven, explains to us that before the throne of God there are *"golden bowls full of incense, which are the prayers of God's people"* (Revelation 5:8). However, not all our prayers have the impression of a nice smelling fragrance, but only the ones which are agreed by God, that is to say those inspired by the Holy Spirit. Flesh, intellectual and self-centered prayers vanish into the atmosphere, because they do not have enough substance to go up. As I often like to say: "They do not go over the ceiling". The motivations of our hearts are essential, because the power of our prayers and their fulfillment depend on them. When Jesus prayed for the resurrection of Lazarus, He addressed the Father and told Him something very interesting: "*__I knew that you always hear me__, but I said this for the benefit of the people standing here, that they may believe that you sent me.*" (John 11:42). All the prayers made by Jesus would receive a positive answer, because He expressed the perfect will of the Father. Likewise, the more we submit to the Holy Spirit, the more *the same mindset as Christ Jesus* is in us (Philippians 2:5), and the more our requests are also in perfect accordance with the will of God. **The more our intimacy with God grows and the more the Holy Spirit can even take us into a dimension in which 100% of our prayers receive fulfillment, because they correspond to needs God wanted to answer.** Our prayers become the oral expression of what was already on his heart, because the intimacy we have developed with Him has an effect in us in such a way that his desires have become our desires. However, God needs a man or woman to be on the front line, which means to pray, to be able to step in "human affairs" and liberate his blessing, or in some cases his judgment. Remember that God having given governance of the Earth to human beings, our prayers enable Him to act legitimately on the Earth, as it is written in this verse: "*The highest heavens belong to the LORD, but the earth he has given to mankind.*" (Psalm 115:16). Conversely, pride closes the doors of heaven on us because "***God opposes the proud but shows favor to the humble***" (1 Peter 5:5). I would like to show you two reasons why God resists proud people, to emphasize the importance of watching over our hearts at all times.

Firstly: The fact that we think we are superior prevents us from being at the service of others and of God. Jesus is a King who became a servant, and He has come to serve, not to be served. (Matthew 20:28). A proud person will not be at the service of others, unless this is in his own interest. Indeed, pride pushes him into getting always interested in himself before the others, and this even in his service at the local church. The Bible corrects us concerning this sort of attitude, by inciting us to see others as being superior to us. Let us look at this verse which clearly explains the importance of watching over our motivations of our actions: *"Do nothing out of selfish ambition or vain conceit. Rather, **in humility value others above yourselves**; not looking to your own interests but each of you to the interests of the others."* (Philippians 2:3-4). Only humbleness gives us the good dispositions of the heart to be helpful to others, contrary to pride, which will always push us to try to attract the looks on us. This is so subtle and hidden inside us that we do not always realize it. Let us look at these two examples to see how it can manifest:

- A worship leader who will try to be noticed by the beauty of her voice, rather than letting herself be fully guided by the Holy Spirit, to bring the assembly before the throne of God.

- A teacher who will try to impress by his knowledge, rather than instructing the believers to see them deeply transformed.

Through these two examples, we see that these two people are at the service of others, but pride actually drives them to be at the service of themselves. This is so subtle that sometimes they do not even realize it, hence the importance of regularly examining our heart, to see what our true motivations are.

<u>Secondly</u>: Pride pushes us to look for our own glory, instead of God's. When God answers our requests, or when He uses us in a particular way and that pride is present in our heart, we tend to believe that it is "thanks to our prayers" or "thanks to our work" that we have succeeded in or obtained such and such thing. It does not mean that we must not work, nor be proud of the work we have done, nor congratulate someone who has been hardworking and rejoice with him. Simply two things have to be remembered, to be protected and always keep a humble heart: *"For it is God who works in you to will and to act in order to fulfill his good purpose"* (Philippians 2:13) and *"Every good and perfect gift is from above, coming down from the Father of the heavenly lights, who does not change like shifting shadows"* (James 1:17). These two verses remind us the importance of always remaining humble, because not only it is God who deposits in us the desire to do such and such thing, but it is also Him who gives us the talent or talents to accomplish it. Add in the action of the Holy Spirit in us and through us to give us the capability. The day when we become aware of that, we realize that we are not the only actors of our success. God kindles in us the will and the making. The Holy Spirit shows us the way to succeed, and He can even in some cases put us in contact with one or several people who will help us in the accomplishment of HIS project (and not ours). And his might helps us stay the course. This awareness enables us to remain humble, and to give glory to God who is the Author of all things. Having been at his service, and the fact that He could have stepped in on the Earth and answered the needs of men through our intermediary is our gratification. The more we are humble and the more God can trust us, because He knows that not only will we not steal His glory, but in addition He will not lose us once we "succeed". I voluntarily put quotation marks, to remind us that success according to society and according to God are completely opposed. Many were close to God when they had nothing and were totally dependent on Him, but wealth, fame or success have finally put an end to their first love and have them forget the One to whom they owe everything. Humbleness preserves our intimacy with God, and protects us against ourselves, since when pride takes too much room, we can become our own god.

3 - Humbleness changes the outlook we have at the others

You may know the expression: "Do not judge a book by its cover". Our level of humbleness influences our openness, and our look to the others. A humble person is generally way more accessible and quicker to listen, even to question himself, than a proud person who thinks he knows everything. A humble person tries to consider people on an equal footing, whereas a proud person will tend to appreciate them according to what they think and how they behave as deemed good. **Humbleness is one of the purest filters, it strips our look of every human consideration and predisposes us to meet new people.** It is solely in a context of trust that even the most closed people allow themselves to open the door of their heart, because they know they will not be judged. Behind a distant attitude can hide rich experiences or unfortunately sad stories, precious treasures or deep injuries. Humbleness enables us to have a listening ear, and to consider people at their right value.

Humbleness is one of the virtues of the character of Christ, and every born-again Christian must, at the image of his Savior, have this quality in him if he really wants to please Him. Jesus has described Himself as being *gentle and humble in heart* (Matthew 11:29). He liked having some closeness with the people He met, and exchanging words with them to let them express the nature of their needs. The very first miracle He accomplished happened during a wedding, during which wine was missing. His mother asked Him to help the newlyweds and, even though his hour had not come yet, He positively answered by transforming water into wine. One day, He went to Zacchaeus, the leader of the publicans (tax collectors) to have a meal. Religious people blamed Him for being in contact with people with a bad reputation. On another day, He took the boat to go to the land of the Gerasenes, to exorcise a legion of demons out of a man. Humbleness would always lead his path, and push Him to be as close as possible to the population and the left behind. It enabled Him to see people not as society could consider them, but with a look full of compassion and love.

Chapter 4
Faithfulness

*"My eyes will be on the faith-
ful in the land, that they may dwell
with me; the one whose walk is
blameless will minister to me."*
(Psalm 101:6)

There was a time when a mere word given, a vow or a handshake, to validate an agreement between two or several people was enough. The promise had a very important value, because it engaged the honor and the reputation of the people who had reached an agreement. People used to have a sense of honor and values, and tried to see to their commitment at best, for they knew that their good or bad reputation would depend on that. However, this state of mind has withered away little by little. As of now, when two parties make a commitment, they establish a contract in due form, with a whole range of clauses to ensure there is no loophole enabling one of the two parties to get rid of its engagement if it came to change one's mind. These last few years, the government has implemented several laws enabling the softening of commercial contracts. In France, real estate buyers now dispose of a ten-day (instead of seven) withdrawal period as part of a sale agreement. Recently, there have also been "non-binding contracts" that make it possible for customers to disengage whenever they wish. Waiting for the anniversary date to break a contract is no longer mandatory as it could have been at a time. This disengaging possibility does not stop here. When taking the Parisian underground, it is no longer surprising to see advertising posters promoting websites lauding extramarital relationships.

Nowadays, the law of commitment has lost all meaning among some people, whether on the marital, sentimental, friendly, professional, personal or on another level, for individual interest has prevailed. Human beings more and more reluctantly accept the strings depriving them of part of their freedom, according to them. This state of mind leads some people to refuse every sort of obligation. But is it that surprising in a society growingly tending to individualism? Is it surprising to see people disengaging as soon as they have "changed their mind", who "no longer want to", or "long for seeing something else"? King Solomon wrote at his time: "*Many claim to have unfailing love, but a faithful person who can find?*" (Proverbs 20:6). If in his day, loyalty already seemed to be a scarcity, how can it be about today? **Over time, the words "trust", "reliability" and "loyalty" have gradually lost their weight, because they have been partly emptied from their meaning, whereas they remain irremovable pillars on which every genuine relationship must be based.**

God likes loyal people, because He is, it is his nature. It reads in the Bible that: "*if we are faithless, he remains faithful, for he cannot disown himself*" (2 Timothy 2:13). That is why when He speaks, He cannot speak in vain, because each of his words commits his Name. His words have repercussions both in our space-time, but also beyond, because every pronounced word activates another dimension. **Every time God speaks, the Holy Spirit is in charge of orchestrating his execution.** We are not always aware of that, but at the sound of his voice, the whole of creation, that is to say the universe, the Earth, the angels and the men (consciously or not) gear up to give life to his words, at the very moment when they have to be executed. God is the master of time and circumstances, and if his promises take a long time to take shape, they will inevitably come to pass, since *it will not return to me empty, but will accomplish what I desire and achieve the purpose for which I sent it* (Isaiah 55:11).

God's faithfulness is visible throughout the history of mankind and this through different ways:

- **His never-failing love**: Salvation is possible for all human beings, despite their failures, and their refusal to accept the helping hand of God: "*For God so loved the world that he gave his one and only Son, that whoever believes in him shall not perish but have eternal life.*" (John 3:16).

- **His blessings**: They are addressed to all human beings, regardless of their condition. God loves men evenly, He does not play favorites, and does not consider them according to their skin color, their social position or their education level. The Bible mentions that "*He causes his sun to rise on the evil and the good, and sends rain on the righteous and the unrighteous.*" (Matthew 5:45)

- **His covenants**: The Bible teaches us that in different moments in history, God concluded covenants with men such as Noah, Abraham, Israel or King David. The covenant is the highest level of commitment between two individuals, it is as strong as the link, the unity which must exist between spouses. God has also concluded a *New Covenant* with men through his Son Jesus Christ. Those who receive Jesus Christ as their Lord and personal Savior benefit from privileges of this New Covenant. They are forgiven their sins, are insured of eternal life and can as for now have direct access to God, as we can see in this verse: *"For this reason Christ is the mediator of a **new covenant**, that those who are called may receive the promised eternal inheritance — now that he has died as a ransom to set them free from the sins committed under the first covenant."* (Hebrews 9:15).

- **His promises**: many of our contemporaries wonder and ask themselves why, if God exists, are there so many wars, violence, injustice, poverty and environmental disasters? God is, of course, not responsible for all these things at all, these being finally only the consequences of the malice of men. His promises to us are far more than excellent, for He tells us: *"For I know the plans I have for you, declares the LORD, plans to prosper you and not to harm you, plans to give you hope and a future."* (Jeremiah 29:11).

Every covenant is governed by both rights and duties. Somebody who enters the framework of the New Covenant benefits from many privileges, but is also submitted to some duties. The man and the woman who accept the requirements of this covenant, and particularly who remain loyal to it, will then enjoy its many promises. Faithfulness is an essential quality to enter God's plans for our life and to know Him intimately. I would like to show you five advantages loyalty to God gives us.

1 - Only faithful people will inherit the crown of glory

Jesus told his disciples one day the story of the man who went on a trip and gave possessions to his servants. He gave five bags of gold to one, two bags to another, and one bag to the third. When he came back, he asked each of them to tell him what they had done with what had been given to them. The one who had had five bags, gave his master five others; the one who had had two, gave his master two others, and the one who had had only one gave the one he had received. The master congratulated the first two servants for their faithfulness by telling them: *"Well done, good and faithful servant! You have been faithful with a few things; I will put you in charge of many things. Come and share your master's happiness!"* (Matthew 25:23). As for the third, he explained that he had buried the bag of gold in the soil, because he was afraid of his master. He told him: *"I knew that you are a hard man, harvesting where you have not sown and gathering where you have not scattered seed"* (v.24). The master blamed him for not having deposited it in the bank, so that it made him earn some interest at least, and he ordered him to be thrown in the darkness outside.

Is it not surprising that the third was so harshly judged, whereas at no moment the master clearly indicated what he expected from his servants? This proves us that the servants knew their master and they knew what his will was, without him needing to remind them of. The two servants who took care of what had been entrusted to them were judged as being good and faithful. "Good" because they managed to make the money yield a profit, and "faithful" because they made the will of their master. Jesus gave the disciples this parable, to explain to them that God has also given talents to each one of us and that the use we make of it will determine the awards we will inherit in heaven, depending on if we have used them for our own glory or for his. **Any person who endeavors to know the will of God for his life and to put to good use the talents he has been entrusted with to reach his goal, is considered as being faithful to his eyes, because he becomes the extension of his arm on the Earth.** In other words, it is as if God intervened in the business of men through this person.

Jesus **is** the mediator between God and men (1 Timothy 2:5), He **is** the image of the invisible God (Colossians 1:15), and He **is** the Word of God (1 John 1:1-3). Everybody was impressed by the way He taught with authority and the numerous miracles He accomplished. Jesus revealed to them the secret of his success. He told them: "*Very truly I tell you, **the Son can do nothing by himself; he can do only what he sees his Father doing, because whatever the Father does the Son also does.***" (John 5:19), and also: "*For I did not speak on my own, **but the Father who sent me commanded me to say all that I have spoken.***" (John 12:49). The success of his earthly ministry was linked to the fact that He was totally dependent on God. That is why at the end of each day, or very early before sunrise, He would withdraw to a desert place to pray to the Father. On this daily meeting, He would receive his instructions for the day, what He had to say, what He had to do, as well as the place where He had to go. Jesus only taught what God prescribed Him to say, and He would only do what God asked Him to do. All those who were in touch with Him would see the Father through Him, without even knowing it, that is why He said to Philip, who wished to see the Father: "*Anyone who has seen me has seen the Father*" (John 14:9). Jesus was the perfect representation of the Father on Earth; He was identical to Him in every respect. He was faithful to Him on all sides, because He is Himself God. He was loyal to Him as to the **character**: faithful in love, in benevolence, in mercy, in empathy, in serving others. He was faithful to

Him in **works**: miracles and healings. He was faithful to Him in **submission,** as it is so well shown in the following verse: "*For I have come down from heaven **not to do my will but to do the will of him who sent me.***" (John 6:38). The success of the ministry of Jesus Christ is explained by his submission and his perfect faithfulness to the Father. Jesus remained faithful to the end, even when in the garden of Gethsemane, He was prey to an unprecedented battle in his thoughts. When He saw the terrible ordeal waiting for Him, his entire self was invaded by anguish, to such an extent that his sweat became like blood lumps (Luke 22:44). Medicine calls this very rare phenomenon hematidrosis. It happens when someone is confronted with extreme anxiety and stress. Alone with the "decision of his life", Jesus did not stop repeating though: "*not as I will, but as you will*" (Matthew 26:39). However, He had the possibility to give up, because his Father had given Him the choice, as He explained it one day to his disciples: "*No one takes it from me, but I lay it down of my own accord. I have authority to lay it down and authority to take it up again. This command I received from my Father.*" (John 10:18). But He chose to remain faithful against all odds to his commitment and his complete submission to the Father, *by **becoming obedient to death** — even death on a cross* (Philippians 2:8). That is why He inherited the Name above all names, and He received all power from the Father in Heaven, on Earth and below Earth.

2 - Faithfulness in small things enables to have bigger ones

The Book of Genesis tells us the story of Joseph who, sold by his brothers, became a slave of Potiphar, an officer of Pharaoh. Potiphar noticed that the Lord was with Joseph, because he was successful in everything he did. So, he decided to entrust him with the management of his house. Unfortunately, Potiphar's wife, who wanted to sleep with Joseph, laid one day false charges against him, offended by his repeated refusals. She accused him of rape, and Joseph was then thrown into prison. It did not take long for the head of the prison to entrust him with the surveillance of all the prisoners, seeing that God was with him. In spite of the betrayal of his brothers and the false charges of Potiphar's wife, Joseph remained faithful to God and honest, **and this is precisely how he passed the test.** God knew He could count on him from this point forward, and entrust him with greater responsibilities, because he had been faithful about small things. Some time later, Pharaoh had a dream that particularly troubled him. He consulted magicians and wise men, but none of them could interpret it for him. The leader of the cupbearers who was imprisoned with Joseph for some time, remembered him and told Pharaoh that he knew somebody able to interpret his dream. Pharaoh summoned him, and not only did Joseph manage to give him the explanation, but he also gave him the strategy to implement to cope with the coming famine. Impressed by his wisdom and his cleverness, Pharaoh decided to designate him number two of Egypt, after him. (Genesis 37:47). Joseph had gone through different ordeals, but because he remained faithful to God despite all of that, God raised him up when He decided to.

This story reminds us of King David's, who originally was a mere shepherd. When he looked after the sheep of his father, he did not hesitate to put his life at risk by fighting the lion and the bear, to snatch them from death. He also displayed bravery when he faced the giant Goliath, and when he fought enemy peoples. It is thanks to his faithfulness in small things that God enabled him later to rule over a whole people.

Jesus taught one day his disciples the following thing: *"Whoever can be trusted with very little can also be trusted with much, and whoever is dishonest with very little will also be dishonest with much."* (Luke 16:10). God will always begin with entrusting us with little tasks, to make us ready, but also to examine the way we deal with them. Some people naturally tend to take very seriously the little responsibilities entrusted to them, and to be involved with zeal, regardless of the fact that their work is well or little considered in the eyes of others. From the moment they are entrusted with a task to achieve, they see to it with seriousness. A man or a woman who can take care of things that can seem worthless for some, is someone who will be trustworthy, when the moment will come to entrust him with greater responsibilities. The "little things" and the "little responsibilities" will have served as a test to observe his behavior and expose the true motivations of his heart. **The sincerity of a person can be seen through the way he behaves, when he knows that nobody looks at him, because the human being tends to adopt an attitude whether he is observed or he knows he is out of sight.**

3 - Our relationship with God and with the others depends on our faithfulness

According to a study, France counts about 130,000 divorces a year and 45% of marriages end up with a divorce[1]. The main cause is infidelity. The married couples have sworn fidelity for the best and for the worst though before the mayor, their relatives, and even before God for some. What has happened? Have they forgotten their vows? The elders will tell you with

---

1. Internet source: www.jurifiable.com, https://www.jurifiable.com/conseil-juridique/droit-de-la-famille/divorce-france-statistiques.

wisdom that passing time is the best way to test fidelity. The years, arguments, financial problems, the coming of one or several children, the putting on weight, the loss of a job, diseases and the trials of life will be the best way to test the resistance of feelings, and check if the promise of fidelity was genuine or if it was merely words. Fidelity is neither an emotion nor a feeling, but a choice. It consists in taking a firm resolution and keeping it whatever the cost.

Fidelity is a token of trustworthiness, dedication and durability. Characteristics that are, you will certainly agree with me about that, increasingly scarce nowadays, in our relationships with others but also with God. Men and women who had a good start with Christ, but who stopped at a given moment on the side of the path, are countless. The problem is not so much to stop, because Christian life is like a long-distance race, and every good runner knows that he may sometimes take a break, to recover and take a breath, to resume with greater intensity. The mistake is to put an end to the race once and for all, even to back out and to return to the starting point. Our earthly pilgrimage is long and chaotic, but let us remain faithful to the end, for the sufferings of the present time are nothing compared to the glory to come.

4 - God knows He can trust faithful people

The emergence of new technologies and social networks offer a wide range of possibilities, but also of entertainments. It has become more and more difficult nowadays to do only one thing at a time, and to remain focused on it until the end. Many people start something and stop even before having finished. Many commit themselves and do not keep their word, say "yes" and do the contrary. Only people who are willful enough to draw away from some entertainment for a while, such as switching off the phone, disconnecting from social networks, taking a break on video games or TV series, will be able to reach the goal they have set themselves. Nevertheless, this requires discipline and some strength of character.

God looks for loyal men and women, trustworthy people who are willing to collaborate with Him to bring answers and solutions to our fellow human beings. Needless to tell you that such people are rare, otherwise how to account for the fact that the world goes so unwell, whereas He has designated his children as being the salt of the Earth and the light of the world? If each one loyally manifested what God called him to, society would certainly be completely different. As long as we will not be found faithful in the mission He has entrusted us with, we will have a part of responsibility in the tragedy which is happening before our eyes. Each of us is called to make this world better, by manifesting love for each other, but also by giving life to what God has deposited in us.

When God finds a faithful person, He has the assurance that He can entrust him with his projects and particularly that he will keep his commitment. Despite the hardships and vagaries of life, he will draw in Himself the sufficient strength to pursue to the end. On examining the life of King David, we have seen that one of the decisive elements that have brought God to choose him was the fact that He saw in him a man who would accomplish all his will. Let us look at this passage again: *"I have found David son of Jesse, a man after my own heart; he will do **everything** I want him to do."* (Acts 13:22). I would like to draw your attention on the indefinite adjective "everything". Only loyal people manage to accomplish **all** the will of God because many people start, but unfortunately very few pursue to the end. But men and women who pass "the test" and are found faithful, are added to the list of people on whom God knows He can count.

A few weeks before writing my first book, the Holy Spirit asked me the following question: "Can I count on you?" Thinking it was my own thoughts, I did not pay attention at the beginning, until the question became more and more insistent. I understood at that moment that it was God. Unwilling to answer directly, I answered with another question: "Why such a question?" He told me: "Because there are very few people on whom I can count." So I remained silent. I took time for reflection to wonder why He addressed me, and particularly where could be the trap… This may make you smile, but I did not want to commit myself without being sure to keep my word. After having pondered for a few minutes, I ended up by saying "yes", but hesitatingly. The conversation ended here; He did not tell me anything else. But two weeks later, He asked me to write the book: "The revelation of God's sons." I then understood that He had asked me this question to know if He could entrust me with this project. Because of the answer I had given, I was from then on bound by my word. Given the extent of work and problems met with, I understood a long time after why He had asked me this question. He wanted to make sure that I would go to the end, and that I would not give up, even if He would give me the ability to achieve his will. God is sovereign, He obviously knows the end before the beginning of our story, but by involving us in the decision-making, through that He shows us that although He is God, He needs our consent and our participation.

5 - Faithfulness is a proof of honesty and a token of trust

The human being exists to live as a community and to be in relationship with others. The couple, the family, the friends, the school, the workplace and society are different circles in which everyone is brought to evolve at different moments of his life, and to build (or not) relationships. In every new meeting, we ourselves decide on the level of involvement we wish to give to this dawning relationship. The sincerity of a relationship will depend on the closeness we develop with the person or the people we rub shoulders with, as well as the place we give them in our life. Every relationship to which we refuse to entirely open up will remain superficial, because there cannot be any true interaction without a real heart to heart from both sides. This requires the acceptance of making oneself vulnerable and trusting the other, which is harder and harder nowadays. Indeed, a lot of people find it difficult to trust and to open up to the other, because of inner injuries linked to a broken friendship, a love breakup, a lie or a betrayal that have strongly affected them. Very few realize that behind some smiles hide deeply ingrained pains, and outer scars are sometimes quite light when compared to soul injuries.

The faithful friend is a precious person, who is preferable to all valuable objects and scores of flatterers. He enables you to be yourself, because he loves you as you are, and when he corrects you, it is always for your sake. Faithfulness in feelings, in commitments, in sincerity and in availability, is vital to build a lasting and genuine relationship. Faithfulness is one of the qualities that particularly pleases the hearts of men and of God, because it is **a proof of honesty and a token of trust.** It is part of the nine attributes of the fruit of the Spirit, as Paul the apostle mentioned in his letter to Galatians: *"But the fruit of* *the Spirit is love, joy, peace, forbearance, kindness, goodness,* **_faithfulness_**, *gentleness and self-control."* (Galatians 5:22-23). Every born-again Christian is supposed to manifest the fruit of the Spirit, thanks to the presence of the Holy Spirit in him. The closer he comes to God and lets Him transform him, the more he is in a position to manifest love, joy, peace and faithfulness. Today more than ever, the world needs faithful men and women people on whom people can count, because there cannot be any true relationship without trust.

ADVICE N°3

Letting all His will happen through you

Chapter 1
King David, a hero according to God

*"For the eyes of the LORD range
throughout the earth to strengthen
those whose hearts are fully committed to him."* (2 Chronicles 16:9)

Several stories in the Bible show us how much a human being is tied to what he sees. One of the most famous ones being very certainly the one in which God asks Samuel to go to Jesse the Bethlehemite, to anoint one of his sons as future king. When arriving on the spot, the prophet asks Jesse to present to him his sons and when he sees them, he immediately thinks it must be Eliab, the eldest son, because he is tall and handsome, and his appearance must probably remind him of King Saul. God interrupts him in his reflection and tells him: *"Do not consider his appearance or his height, for I have rejected him. The LORD does not look at the things people look at. **People look at the outward appearance, but the LORD looks at the heart**."* (1 Samuel 16:7). The fact that the physical beauty of King Saul, David and Eliab, is repeatedly mentioned in the Bible, encourages us to wonder whether this was a necessary criterion to be king. Although the Bible does not really give us any explanation about this subject, we know that people are more easily influenced by people to whom they are somewhat attracted.

Humanly speaking, Eliab should have been chosen as king, for as the eldest son, he benefited from a rank and privileges superior to his brothers', as the Hebrew tradition requires. Indeed, at the death of the father, the eldest son received a double part of the inheritance, as well as the title of head of household. In addition, the name Eliab means "God is a father", which may suggest that he was probably a man who feared God. Prophet Samuel still submits to God and keeps reviewing the six other brothers, but without succeeding to find among them the one chosen by God. Then he asks Jesse if all his sons are really there, but he answers him that the youngest is absent, because he tends the sheep. Samuel asks to fetch him, and as soon as he sees him, God tells him straight away that he has been chosen to be king. Then the prophet pours anointing oil on the young man, who is immediately seized by the Spirit of God (1 Samuel 16:13).

Let us take a moment to think about this story and let us try to understand why the choice of God turned towards David rather than Eliab. To have a better understanding of his choice, it is essential to remind the historical context of the time. It is noteworthy that before having Saul as king, the Hebrew people were governed by judges. The judges were heads in charge with the administration of their province, and with the restoration of order in a crisis situation. Charismatic judges such as Gideon, Othniel, Jephthah, Samson and the prophet Samuel were empowered with the Spirit of God, who would help them carry out their mission. One day, the elders of Israel came to visit prophet Samuel, who was the last of the judges, and told him they wished to have a king to govern them, like the other nations. Samuel took counsel with God, who answered him: *"Listen to all that the people are saying to you; **it is not you they have rejected, but they have*** *rejected me as their king*." (1 Samuel 8:7). God would lead his people and give them victory over their enemies through judges He had established and clothed with his power. By rejecting his mode of governance, the people would not only reject Samuel, but also God. However, God "accepted" their request and asked prophet Samuel to consecrate Saul as king. Let us have a look at the way the Bible presents him: "*There was a Benjamite, **a man of standing**, whose name was Kish son of Abiel, the son of Zeror, the son of Bekorath, the son of Aphiah of Benjamin. Kish had a son named Saul, as handsome a young man as could be found anywhere in Israel, and he was a head taller than anyone else*." (1 Samuel 9:1-2). Saul was undoubtedly impressive with his physical appearance, for the author of the book of Samuel takes great care emphasizing this aspect a second time in another passage (1 Samuel 10:23). Likewise, the expression "man of standing" was used to describe brave men and heroes on the battlefield. Saul, who was the son of a warrior, had also probably inherited this quality, as proved by the battle he won against the Ammonites, as well as all the following others (1 Samuel 11). Despite his predispositions, Saul failed in his role of king because of his character, which eventually drove him to destroy his destiny. Character is the capital ingredient in the life of an individual, because from it directly depends success or failure. John Wooden, considered as the greatest basketball American university coach, said one day: "*Ability may get you to the top, but it takes character to keep you there*". His durability as a coach, his honors, his experience, his successes, his failures as well as the different career paths of his former pupils clearly enabled him to make this statement. Talent can make you achieve great things, but your character enables you to make the right or wrong choices, and finally determines the guidance you give to your existence. In order to have a better grasp of this aspect, I would like us to compare the profile of King Saul and of King David, to clearly understand why one failed and the other one succeeded.

1 - King Saul

- **Flaws in the character of King Saul**

When we take time to study the life of King Saul, we can see that several flaws appear concerning his character. I would like to highlight three of them, to help you have a better understanding of the reasons why this man, who had been chosen by God, failed.

- The disobedience of Saul

King Saul unhesitatingly disobeyed twice the recommendations of prophet Samuel. The very first time, Prophet Samuel asked him to wait for him seven days before joining him and telling him what he had to do thereafter (1 Samuel 10:8). Saul waited seven days, but when he saw that the prophet was late to come and that the people would start scattering, he took the decision of offering himself a burnt offering to God. On arriving, the prophet was unpleasantly surprised to see that Saul had disobeyed him. As he asked him to give an explanation, Saul answered him:

> *"When I saw that the men were scattering, and that you did not come at the set time, and that the Philistines were assembling at Mikmash, I thought, 'Now the Philistines will come down against me at Gilgal, and I have not sought the LORD's favor.' So I felt compelled to offer the burnt offering." "You have done a foolish thing," Samuel said. "You have not kept the command the Lord your God gave you; if you had,*

he would have established your
kingdom over Israel for all time.”
(1 Samuel 13:11-13)

On seeing the people walking away, Saul took fright and gave a burnt offering in Prophet Samuel's stead. That was all it took for God to choose to withdraw him royalty straight away. His act clearly demonstrated a lack of reliability, because if he had been able to disobey that easily a first time, he could do it again a second time. This is what happened by the way, since right after this episode, he definitely disobeyed a second time. In fact, as prophet Samuel had asked him to exterminate the city of Amalek and everything belonging to him, he had it all his own way by sparing the king and the best cattle. When he went there, Prophet Samuel found out a second time that he had disobeyed him (1 Samuel 15:13-15). Instead of simply acknowledging his mistake, Saul explained the fact that he had kept the best cattle to offer it in sacrifice to God.

These two incidents clearly show us that God could no longer trust such a man, because given his responsibilities, his decisions had repercussions not only on him, but on the people as a whole. But God could not allow Himself to take such a risk, because He needed someone trustworthy to be able to govern his people and to bring them into the dimension He wished. When somebody is faithful in small things, he can be entrusted to bigger ones without worry, but if he takes his little commitments lightly, he will act the same way when his responsibilities increase, as it is so well said in the following verse: *“Whoever can be trusted with very little can also be trusted with much, and whoever is dishonest with very little will also be dishonest with much.”* (Luke 16:10). The specificity of Saul was that he had been propelled king without having demonstrated the ability before. His reaction facing the people revealed that he had neither the experience nor the character for that, it unveiled the state of his heart in broad daylight.

However, I would like to draw your attention on the reasons leading him to disobey, because our analysis would be incomplete if we only settle on these two reactions. In fact, if we take time to think about the reason why he reacted this way, we realize that his behavior was mainly guided by fear. In the first case, it was about the fear of finding himself alone when he realized that the people were starting to scatter. His reaction shows us that he trusted men more than God. His attitude suggests that he certainly believed that his victory was linked to the number of soldiers rather than the active and protective hand of God. In the second case, he and the people took the initiative of sparing the king as well as the cattle. His doing shows us once again fear, but this time regarding the people. Yet, it was his role, as a king, to tell the people what God required from him. Instead of that, he joined up to the side of the majority by refusing to take a clear position and to tell them what the will of God was. As for the first time, the large number got the better of him. When we take time to read his story carefully, we realize that this fear was indeed present from the beginning, because when Samuel wanted to anoint him as king, he did not find him because he had hidden among the supplies (1 Samuel 10:22). Despite his stature and his fighting qualities, he revealed a lack of self-confidence, but also of trust in God. It is when he was elevated at the highest rank that this personality trait finally entailed his fall. If he had been tested as David was, he would have learned then how to put his trust in God only and not in him or in the people. Fear would have had no longer any grip on him and, like Paul the apostle, he could also have said: *"If God is for us, who can be against us?"* (Romans 8:31).

This observation pushes me to ask you a question: which is the personality trait that causes you trouble in your relationships with the others, your professional career, the achievement of your plans and/or your relationship with God? You have to know that some personality traits have such an influence on our attitude, that as long as we refuse to treat them, our life will seem like blocked. Indeed, not only can they prevent us from grasping the blessings God has for us, but they can also bring about our fall, if we accede to greater responsibilities in the future or to a greater fame.

- **The pride of Saul**

After having gained several victories, King Saul decided to erect a monument for himself (1 Samuel 15:12). By acting this way, he would copy the customs of neighboring peoples, some of them considering their king as a god on Earth. When he learned that, Prophet Samuel blamed him for that, by regretting he had lost the humbleness he had at the beginning. He told him: "*You were once small in your own eyes, did you not become the head of the tribes of Israel? The Lord anointed you king over Israel.*" (1 Samuel 15:17). Saul had become proud, because he certainly thought that his victories were the result of his own actions. His pride is also explained by the fear and the lack of trust he had when he started out, because from then on, he considered that he had become somebody important.

- **The jealousy of Saul**

After having defeated the giant Goliath, David joined the army of King Saul. He was very much appreciated by the people, because he was at the head of the army, he would win many victories and the Lord was with him. One day, on coming back from the battlefield, women improvised a song in his honor: "*Saul has slain his thousands, and David his tens of thousands.*" (1 Samuel 18:7). From that day on, Saul looked very unfavorably on the popularity of David, and it was enough for jealousy to reach his heart. From then on, he would no longer see him as a brother in arms, but as a rival. His resentment was such that he finally hated him, and tried to kill him on several occasions.

• **Conclusion on Saul**

This quick overview of King Saul's life has enabled us to have a better insight of who he was, and to understand the reasons which finally brought him to fail. Consequently, we have a better understanding of the reasons why the selection criteria of the next king had to be different from Saul's. The latter would no longer be based on his appearance, his charisma and his leading qualities, but also and particularly on the state of his heart. God needed to find a heart in which He was sure to have the first place, so that the ambitions He had for his people may take shape through this person. He found the quality He was looking for in the person of a young shepherd named David. These qualities may not have been visible at first sight for the people who focus on what strikes the sight and draws attention, but the One who searches the heart and examines the mind (Jeremiah 17:10), perceived in him the characteristics so wanted. Nobody would have bet a coin on this young man, not even his father and his brothers who had thought it unnecessary to think of him on the invitation of prophet Samuel. That is why I would like to show you what was so special about David for God to see in him a man according to his heart.

2 - David: a kind of hero according to God

After four hundred and thirty years of slavery in Egypt, forty years in the desert, several battles to conquer the Promised Land, periods of peace at times and war with their neighbors at other times, especially because of their disobedience to God, the people of Israel was always late entering the great project that God had planned for them. His dream was his people to become a great nation to influence the peoples around and to bring them to his knowledge, to be a reference in the area on the economic, political, cultural and religious level. To carry out this large-scale project, it was necessary that his people obey Him, to enjoy the blessings He had kept for them, and it is precisely in this respect that Saul failed. So, He needed a man whose heart was totally submitted to Him, so that his will may perfectly come about through him. However, it seems that so very few people have this sort of profile, that God was compelled to look for one, as we can see in this exchange between prophet Samuel and King Saul, when Samuel announced to Saul that God had forsaken him: "*The Lord **has sought out** a man **after his own heart** and appointed him ruler of his people, **because you have not kept** the Lord's command.*" (1 Samuel 13:14). A similar verse in the book of Acts adds a detail, but not an insignificant one, here is what is said: "*I have found David son of Jesse, **a man after my own heart; he will do everything I want him to do**.*"(Acts 13:22).

When we look at these two verses, it clearly appears that **the main element God looks for in a person is the heart**. Given that his choice fell on David, we can legitimately wonder why this young man was so special for God to be interested in him. Comparing these two verses gives us part of the answer. In the first one, God rejects Saul because of his disobedience, and in the second one we can see that the main element He looks for in a person is precisely his obedience. Making the will of God is one, otherwise THE essential criterion to really please Him. Although David was not perfect, he would try to make the will of God. Let us look a little more closely to what characterized him.

- The personality of David

The life of King David has quite an important part in the Old Testament, since it covers the two books of Prophet Samuel. On reading them, we learn how this simple shepherd, the youngest of seven brothers, was chosen to be king, to the surprise of all. We do not know his exact age at that moment, but we know that several years, probably over a dozen, elapsed before he acceded to the throne, at the age of 30. During all this time, David went through different phases that enabled him to build his character, to strengthen his relationship with God and to surround himself with trustworthy people. Contrary to King Saul who instantly became king, these transition years prepared him to assume his royal functions to come. That is the reason why he succeeded as a king, and during his reign God could make his people a nation. Several noteworthy events characterized his life and explain who he was, and especially the person he has become.

Here are some of them:

- His victory against the giant Goliath testifies of his <u>courage</u> and his <u>determination</u> (1 Samuel 17)

- The many struggles he has won reveal his <u>ability to fight</u> and his <u>stature of military leader</u> (1 Samuel 18:5, 12-16)

- His friendship with Jonathan reveals his <u>loyalty</u> and his <u>righteousness</u> (1 Samuel 20)

- His unwavering respect towards Saul, even though the latter tried on several occasions to kill him, shows his <u>loyalty</u> and his <u>integrity</u>, even though David also had the opportunity to do so. (1 Samuel 19-11, 19-24; 24:5-8)

- His ability to rally his brothers to his cause, as well as to turn simple creditors and discontent people into valiant heroes, show his <u>influence</u> and his <u>leadership ability</u>. (1 Samuel 22:1-2; 23:8-39)

- His tendency to always consult God before making an important choice reveals his <u>complete submission to God</u>.

- His will to build the Temple of God proves us <u>his love and his heart towards the Lord</u> (2 Samuel 7)

As seen earlier, it is the Holy Spirit who has given him the ability to take up all these challenges. Even if he was a man according to the heart of God, we must keep in mind that David was a human being and that he was not perfect. Like everyone else, he too has committed mistakes, some of them being mentioned here, to remove all complex that could have taken place in your heart, as you were reading his history:

- The transportation of the Ark of the Covenant to Jerusalem: David had the Ark of the Covenant put on a cart, and he and his people walked towards Jerusalem. On the way, Uzzah touched the Ark of the Covenant to steady it and to prevent it from falling. Although his gesture was benevolent, the wrath of God struck him and he died because the transportation of the Ark was exclusively restricted to the Levites. (2 Samuel 6)

- The Israeli army counting: David decided one day to count the number of his soldiers. His decision entailed the anger of God, because this implicitly meant that David trusted their number, rather than on the fact that the Lord was by their side. (2 Samuel 24)

- The adultery with Bathsheba: David was in the palace, whereas his army had gone to the battlefield. One night, he saw a woman bathing alone. He summoned her and slept with her. She was the wife of Uriah, one of his soldiers. When he learned that she was pregnant, he asked his officers to put his husband in the midst of the fight. Uriah was killed during the battle. (2 Samuel 11)

- **A heart of shepherd**

God chose David, a mere shepherd, because He needed somebody able to take care of his people. His qualities and his heart pleased God, for he was not only looking for a charismatic leader, a brave warrior, but also a man who takes care of his people and who fears His Name. The choice of a shepherd is consequently not so insignificant as it might seem at first glance, as shows us the following verse: *"He chose David his servant and took him from the sheep pens; from tending the sheep **he brought him to be the shepherd of his people Jacob, of Israel** his inheritance. And **David shepherded them with integrity of heart; with skillful hands he led them**."* (Psalm 78:70-72). By becoming king, David became the shepherd of the people of

Israel. The time he spent with his father's sheep had somehow prepared him to take care of a huge people later. By the way, he is not the only one in this case. Remember that after having killed an Egyptian, Moses fled in the desert where he stayed forty years as a shepherd. Moses, who had been bred up in the palace of Pharaoh and who had benefited from the education of a prince, also went through "the school of shepherds" where he learned humbleness, patience, and service. These qualities enabled him to take care of a people so important and rebellious. The shepherd takes on a very strong symbolic character in the Bible, since Jesus defines Himself as being *the good shepherd*, and those who make the choice of following Him become his sheep (John 10:11). The role of King David and of Moses in the Old Testament is essential, because they represent in a way the Messiah to come. Those two men were admittedly not perfect, but the Messiah to come would be perfect in all things. Look at the similarity between these two verses, the first one presenting David and the second one Jesus Christ:

David:

"(…) *I have found David son of Jesse, a man after my own heart; **he will do everything I want him to do**.*" (Acts 13:22)

Jesus:

"*Then I said, 'Here I am — it is written about me in the scroll — **I have come to do your will, my God**.*'" (Hebrews 10:7)

Once again, we can see that one of the major elements characterizing a man or a woman according to the heart of God is the desire to make the will of God. By coming on the Earth, Jesus also made the choice of completely submitting to God and of making not his will, but his Father's.

- **The relationship of David with God in seven points**

The Book of Psalms is widely considered as one of the nicest books in the Bible. King David, who is the main author, unveils to us the greatness of God, His power, His love, His wisdom, His creativity, His faithfulness, His righteousness, His kindness and His protection. It also shows us several aspects of King David, who appears at times as a worshiper, a warrior full of bravery, but also as a weak man, anxious, abandoned and persecuted. This prophetic book shows us both the greatness and the power of God, but also the human being in all his aspects. One undeniable thing that stands out is the intimate relationship King David had developed with the Lord. David was thoroughly dependent on God, who took him out of herds, established him as king, gave him victory over all his enemies and made his name great on Earth. David was so grateful towards God, and he had such love for Him, that one day he decided to build a temple for Him (1 Samuel 7). God was particularly moved by this attention, but He told him through prophet Nathan that he would not build the Temple, because his hands were covered with the blood of war, but his son Solomon would. Let us have a look at a few aspects of this very strong relationship that existed between King David and God, and why God considered him as being a man according to his heart. This will help us have a better understanding of what God would like to see in each one of us.

1. David was a true worshiper:
"You, God, are my God, earnestly I seek you; I thirst for you, my whole being longs for you, in a dry and parched land where there is no water. I have seen you in the sanctuary and beheld your power and your glory." (Psalm 63:1-2)

2. David was a man of prayer:
"I rise before dawn and cry for help; I have put my hope in your word." (Psalm 119:147)

3. David liked meditating on the Word of God:
"Your word is a lamp for my feet, a light on my path." (Psalm 119:105)

4. David would consult God:
"He inquired of the LORD, saying, "Shall I go and attack these Philistines?" The Lord answered him, "Go, attack the Philistines and save Keilah." (1 Samuel 23:2)

5. David was aware of the prescience of God:
"You know when I sit and when I rise; you perceive my thoughts from afar. You discern my going out and my lying down; you are familiar with all my ways. Before a word is on my tongue you, LORD, know it completely." (Psalm 139:2-4)

6. David was aware of the importance of the Holy Spirit:
"Where can I go from your Spirit? Where can I flee from your presence? If I go up to the heavens, you are there; if I make my bed in the depths, you are there. If I rise on the wings of the dawn, if I settle on the far side of the sea, even there your hand will guide me, your right hand will hold me fast." (Psalm 139:7-10).

7. David had God for protector
"The LORD is my rock, my fortress and my deliverer; my God is my rock, in whom I take refuge, my shield and the horn of my salvation, my stronghold." (Psalm 18:2)

- **Conclusion**

When we compare King David's story with King Saul's, we can see the appearance of two types of profiles. Saul symbolizes men and women of power in a way, who like using their position to privilege their personal interests. Many gain access to high positions with good intentions, but they end up forgetting their commitments, beguiled by the splendor of power. Saul began with God but unfortunately, he ended without Him. Conversely, David represents the people who first and foremost look for making the will of God. Despite his weaknesses, God considered him as a hero, as we can see in this verse:

> *"Once you spoke in a vision to your devoted ones and said, I have endowed one who is mighty [a hero, giving him the power to help—to be a champion for Israel]; I have exalted one chosen from among the people. I have found David my servant; with my holy oil have I anointed him, with whom my hand shall be established and ever abide; my arm also shall strengthen him."* (Psalms 89:19-21)

Is it not something extraordinary to be considered a "hero" by God himself? If God described him this way, it is not only because of his numerous victories, because it is God who would give him domination over his enemies, but rather because of his heart and his obedience. Indeed, the main thing that interests God in a man and a woman is their obedience, for it is a sign showing that He is the master of their life.

Chapter 2
Having the correct perspective

"Set your minds on things
above, not on earthly things."
(Colossians 3:2)

Lying on his bed, Mark strives to keep his eyes open. His wife, his three children and their partners, as well as their children and a few close friends are present. Although they were all prepared, they have difficulty hiding their emotion. Mark looks at them tenderly, then with a barely audible voice, but which seems to resonate in all the room since the silence is so deafening, he tells them in a sigh: "good bye". As his eyes slowly close, everybody understands that what they feared most has just happened. Tears stream down on faces, everybody hugs, and his wife bursts in tears. Mark has just left them. He had a happy life and left surrounded by those he loved. As emotion is at its peak, nobody doubts for a single moment about what is underway on the other side. The spirit of Mark has just left his body, and is taken to a speed superior to the light towards his final destination. His carnal envelope is lying on the bed, but his spiritual body is propelled to a place totally unknown to him. His race slows down little by little, while a force attracts him to a dazzling light. As he gets closer, a strong anxiety seizes him, for he feels so unworthy of the purity. Finally, he stands still, and suddenly he sees his life flashing by before him down to the smallest detail, from the day of his birth up to the day of his death. Rational and a convinced atheist, Mark realizes that there is life after death. Without him being able to explain the reason, he knows deep within him that the values that have led his life are radically contrary to the ones dominating in this place, for they seem so perfect and unalterable. All of a sudden, he is seized by dread, when he understands what his final destination will be.

This story reminds us that we will all have to go before the Creator one day or another, and that every one of us will have to answer to Him at that moment. Everything that will have led our life, driven our thoughts, our words and our actions, will then be confronted to the holiness of God. The importance we used to give to our work, our nice house, our social status, our projects, our trips, our material goods, will suddenly seem quite pointless before his reality. Many people will realize at this very moment that everything that would take up the first place in their heart had taken the place that should have been kept for Him. Many will try to present their good deeds to justify the fact that they are good people, but only the revelation of their heart's hidden intentions will enable to consider whether their actions are worthy of approval from God or not. The most important in the eyes of God is not so much what we do, but rather the person we are. Human being does not have to define what he considers as being good or bad, right or wrong, but God does. Because, in the same way the good tree bears good fruit, a bad tree can inevitably give bad ones only.

There were about thirty Chiefs of State gathered for the funerals of the former president of France Jacques Chirac, on September 30, 2019; what could they think about? When looking at his coffin, in this church of Saint-Sulpice, what could they say to themselves? During his homily, the Archbishop of Paris did not fail to remind that all men were equal before death. The Anglican priest John Wesley said one day: *"I value all things only by the price they shall gain in eternity."* As long as we are on the Earth, it is essential to keep in mind at all times what the real priority of things is, as well as their importance, not from a human point of view, but rather with a perspective coming from God. In fact, what can seem important to us today, will appear pointless to us once we will be on the other side, if we have not been able to have the right perspective. At this moment, we will certainly really regret the way we have lived and given priority to some things.

In France, life expectancy is 80 years on average for men and 85 years for women. This length of time, however long it may be, does not even equal the size of a speck of dust compared to the stretch of the universe. When someone grows old and sees the very first wrinkles appear on his face, he realizes at this moment how time flies by and how much it is precious. The Creator opened the chapter of humanity mankind with these first three words: "In the beginning". This way, every human being is submitted to the clock of God, until the moment when he leaves the Earth to enter eternity. Some reach the age He had determined for them, whereas some others leave the Earth prematurely, because of a dramatic event that has stolen their years. The seconds, minutes, hours, weeks, months and years lose their omnipotence before infinity, since their role is limited to our temporal dimension only. Understanding the power of time is essential to choose correctly the way we enjoy it, because no one can stop it, nor even slow it. But everyone must be aware that the person he becomes between his "birth" and his "death", will definitely determine the place where he will spend his "eternity".

When we are young, we think we are immortal: I am handsome, I am pretty, eternal youth. No matter how beautiful we are, it will sooner or later lose its radiance. Just like the flower, a young girl who liked to play on her beauty also ends up withering when the end of the season comes. She who would take pleasure in seeing boys turning around when she passed by, has trouble in her old age finding someone willing to help her carry her heavy shopping bags. The haughty and contemptuous man ends his old days with loneliness as his only company, his appalling character having driven away the few people who used to surround him. The riches proudly sported by the great and the good, symbols of their success and their social status, become quite pointless when the pleasure they would bring no longer exists and when finally arrives the end of their existence. Such is life. Earthly things just last for a while, only memories can follow the human being up to his eternity. Some will give him great joy and pride. Conversely, regret, sadness or even indefinable anxiety for some others. There is nothing worse than regrets for the human being: "If only" and "Why?", "If only I had known!", "Why didn't I listen?", "Why didn't I say: I love you?", "Why have I refused the extended hand from God to me?". Here are some of the sentences haunting some people when they reach their final destination, or when an unexpected situation steals their joy and destroys their certainties.

All human beings will have to appear before God one day. When we find ourselves before Him, the memory of everything we have lived will immediately come back to our mind. We will be instantly aware of our state without God needing to say even a single word. His reality will suddenly become ours, and everything that had been misrepresented by the human system and what we had taken in as being true will then be confronted with His truth. The personal convictions of many people will be so shaken, that they will have, for a short moment, the feeling that the life they had lived may have only been a dream after all. The context in which they have lived all their life has determined their conscience of reality, but at that moment, the revelation they will have will be so superior to all they have known previously, that they will wonder how they did not have been aware of earlier. A countless number of people will then find themselves before the greatest disillusion they have ever known. Many will not accept their responsibility and will put the blame on the others, by rebuking institutions, scientists, society and the State to have hidden to them the truth according to them. Their accusations will quickly be swept away, when the memory of all the opportunities that have come up to them comes back to them, but they have never been able to take them. Others will be angry at themselves, remembering that a neighbor, a workmate, a friend or a stranger in the street had told them about, but they had not paid any attention, because of their certainties that prevented them from believing. At that moment, everything on which they had built their life will collapse in an instant, like a house of cards. A fright and a strong feeling of guilt will invade all of their self on realizing that they have completely missed out. On the contrary, others will be overwhelmed by a huge bliss on seeing at last what they had put all their hopes for. Rejection and jeering were finally nothing before the glory waiting for them from now on.

By dint of constantly focusing our attention on things from below, we take the risk of forgetting to look towards the sky, except for admiring its turquoise blue expanse. Many people are dazzled by the beauty of the rainbow, but very few know that it is the sign of an alliance made by God with men. The symbol which only appears from time to time, is yet used to remind us that although being on the Earth, another reality also exists. There are two worlds: the first is natural and the second is spiritual, one is visible and the other is invisible. Very few people are aware of that, because society has deliberately chosen to squeeze God out, by concealing Him from textbooks and dismissing Him from our construction as individuals. The emotion sparked off by the cathedral of Notre-Dame de Paris fire, which occurred on April 15, 2019, at the height of Easter, showed us to what extent the spiritual side echoes in the heart of the French though, as long as a building representing them is concerned. The information has spanned the globe, pushing thousands of people to engage in private prayer before the cathedral or in churches, because the need to commune together was stronger than everything. Believers as non-believers were affected by this sad news. For a short while, millions of French lifted up their eyes to the sky, before going back to their daily bustle. What does this event reveal to us? It reminds us that each thing has an end, but the necessity to connect with the Creator remains in the heart of the human being. This need, which seems totally absent when everything is fine, comes back to the point whenever a particular event shakes our certainties. This proves us that finally it is not that far, but it is choked by concerns of the modern world. The approach people can have of God and of life in general is finally merely a question of perspective, and the latter depends on whether we have received the revelation of God or not.

1 - Understanding the spiritual world and discerning the spirits

Understanding the spiritual world enables us to have a better comprehension of the society in which we live. The Bible teaches us that two worlds exist: the visible world and the invisible world: *"By faith we understand that the universe was formed at God's command, so that what is seen was not made out of what was visible."* (Hebrews 11:3). The visible world was created from the invisible world, so that the invisible world existed before the visible world. The Bible does not tell us much concerning this universe hidden to physical senses. However, we know that in the image of the physical world, the spiritual world is also governed by laws. The spiritual world is made up of angels of God, but also of fallen angels commonly called demons. The angels of God are entitled to step in the "affairs of men", notably towards born-again Christians. On several occasions in the Bible, we see angels bringing a specific message to some people, ensuring their protection or fighting in favor of men and women of God (cf. Daniel 10:13). Angels are in charge of wielding a ministry towards saints:

> *"To which of the angels did God ever say, "Sit at my right hand until I make your enemies a footstool for your feet"? Are not all angels ministering spirits sent to serve those who will inherit salvation?"*
> (Hebrews 1:13-14)

The Bible also says that: *"The angel of the LORD encamps around those who fear him, and he delivers them."* (Psalm 34:7). Consequently, we know that there is at least one angel on the side of those who fear God. Some people, depending on their ministry and on the spiritual dimension in which they progress, can have several angels attributed to them. The angels are by our side to protect us, but also to help us accomplish the mission God entrusted us with.

One day, a pastor told us a story to explain to us the importance of speaking in tongues, and the fact that this could in some cases activate the angelic ministry. One evening, after a prayer meeting, a young woman was going back home on a moped, when a car cut in on her and suddenly stopped before her. Four men got out of the vehicle and went towards her. As they were coming closer to her, they suddenly stopped as if there seemed to be something behind her. Overcome by panic, they rushed to their car and went away at full speed. The young woman ended up alone and there was nothing behind her. At the same moment, the pastor who had led the prayer meeting had reached home, and as he was about to have dinner, the Holy Spirit pushed him to pray in tongues for about twenty minutes. He did not really understand the reason why, but he could not help it. The day after, as he was in church, a brother came to see him and told him that during the evening on going back home, he was pushed to speak in tongues. They realized that they had both prayed at the same moment. Then, the young woman came into the church and told them the anecdote she lived the day before, in the evening. The two men then understood that God had used them to pray and that angels had been released to rescue her, hence the terror that gripped them all of a sudden.

Demons also intervene in the "affairs of men", not to serve them, but to destroy them. All human beings, believers or not, are protected from demonic forces by spiritual laws established by God. Demons cannot affect a man or a woman who submits to the principles of God. Conversely, anybody who transgresses them, consciously or not, risks satanic attacks.

What are the things that can open demonic spiritual doors and give the devil-free access into somebody's life, you may say? There are so many that a whole book to describe them would be needed, but here are some of them: occultism, esotericism, witchcraft, magic, clairvoyance, yoga, idolatry, some consecrated objects, some music, some fragrances, some books, some movies, some sexual practices, affiliation to satanic secret societies, all practices calling on spiritual forces and energies, etc. Obedience to the laws and principles of God allows for individuals to be protected and to give no occasion at all to the devil and to his demons to come in our life and destroy it. If God demands our obedience, it is because He wishes to protect us and ensure our happiness. A lot of people consider that the Bible is an obsolete book, totally out of step with our time. They prefer living "freely", without any constraint, until the day when the semblance of freedom closes on them, like a prison. Voluntarily or not, they have broken a spiritual principle and have given an admission ticket to a demon who, after having sometimes provided them with an illusionary pleasure, ends up becoming their worst torturer.

Lucifer, which means angel of light, is the name Satan used to bear before he rebelled against God, and was expelled from Heaven with one third of the angels who were under his governance (Revelation 12:4). From that day on, his main goal is to destroy the creation of God. Demons, also called unclean spirits in the Bible, are fallen angels who were rejected from Heaven with Lucifer. They are bodiless spiritual beings, and cannot interact on the Earth. But it is necessary to have a physical body to act in the physical world. The human being is also a spirit, but as for him, he has a soul and a body available. The human body is a precious element in the eyes of demons, for if they manage to take possession, this gives them a "physical existence" on the Earth. That is the reason why demons try by any means to enter bodies of human beings or animals. Their goal is not only to destroy individuals, but also to be able to interact with the physical world. In the third Book of Genesis, we can see that Satan entered the body of a snake, because he needed a physical body to make his thought materialize and talk to Eve. God had told Man: *"Be fruitful and increase in number; fill the earth and subdue it. Rule over the fish in the sea and the birds in the sky and over every living creature that moves on the ground."* (Genesis 1:28). By obeying Satan, Adam and Eve believed his words, and placed themselves under his authority de facto. It is in this way that they lost governance of the Earth, by giving it in to the devil who has become, from then on, the god of this world. That is why, after Jesus fasted forty days and forty nights in the desert, the devil tempted Him by telling Him: *"I will give you all their authority and splendor; **it has been given to me**, and I can give it to anyone I want to."* (Luke 4:6)

To carry out their actions, unclean spirits need to enter a body, to govern the individual from the inside, and act on the Earth through it. They can also act from the outside by influencing his thoughts, so that he accepts them by thinking they are his, and unknowingly accomplishes the will of one of several demons. When a demon possesses the spirit of an individual, it is generally what is called a demonic possession. When a demon takes action inside a body, but does not possess his spirit, we will rather speak of demonization, or demonic oppression. A born-again Christian cannot be possessed, because his spirit belongs to God, and it is the living place of the Holy Spirit. By contrast, a non-believer can be the victim of a demonic possession, depending on the access he has given to one or several demons, consciously or not. It can also be familiar spirits in some cases, that is to say unclean spirits taking action on a whole family from generation to generation.

I would like to share with you two stories in order to illustrate my point. The first one will give you a better understanding of the demonic spiritual world, if you still have doubts about the existence of these unclean spirits. The second one will show you to what extent we have to be more and more watchful nowadays in some of our choices.

I have a very good friend who works as an elevator mechanic. One evening, he is called for an elevator breakdown in a prestigious banking establishment in Paris in the Opéra district. He knows this place quite well for he has serviced there on several occasions. He does not like going there very much because he feels a weird atmosphere whenever he goes to the basement. The security guards who work on site do not like going to the basement either because they also have the impression of the oppressiveness in the atmosphere. That day, a security guard goes there with him. It is the first time he goes there with him. On reaching the machinery, the man tells him: "I can see an angel above your head." My friend starts smiling because he is a born-again Christian. He tells him: "What do you mean, you can see an angel?". The guard answers: "Yes, I can see an angel. Right here, above your head. There's a light, I know it's an angel." My friend asks him then: "How is that possible? Can you see in the spiritual world?" The agent explains to him that he has a demon in him who gives him some powers, among them the ability to see in the spiritual world. He goes on by saying that his workmates do not like going to the basement, because they do not feel comfortable, but it is normal, because there are lots of demons. As for him, he prefers doing his round by himself, because he sees them, but they can't do anything to him. After having repaired the elevator, my friend had him listen to the message of a pastor on YouTube, which explained the spiritual world and the dangerous nature of demons. The security guards had tears in his eyes. He told him that sometimes the unclean spirit would take possession of him suddenly and that he would become violent to the point where he can beat his companion. Even his little daughter was scared to come closer to him, as if she would feel something. My friend then offered him to get rid of this unclean spirit, but he refused by explaining that he had inherited it from his grandmother and that he would give him a certain power.

Kanda and his wife Maïté were on holidays in the United States. One evening, a friend invited them to attend a prayer meeting. There were about fifteen people, among whom a grunge-dressed young woman in her twenties. What drew

Kanda's attention was not so much her clothing outfit, but the fact that she had a strange behavior. She was moving strangely and seemed completely elsewhere. At the end of the meeting, the pastor asked Kanda if he would pray for the young girl, because she was apparently sick. She had stomach pains. Kanda accepted and as he was about to pray, he realized that she was blind. Her attitude growingly intrigued him, because she would say odd things. On observing her, he had the impression that it was rather about a demonic possession. He asked her mother if she had always been like that, and she explained to him that she used to be normal, but her behavior had suddenly changed since they had gone to the cinema to watch a horror movie. She went on by explaining that she knew that it might seem strange to bring a blind person to the cinema, but it was for the sake of going out and also because it was her favorite series (Twilight). Kanda questioned the young girl to understand if anything in particular had happened for her behavior to become that strange. She said that during the film, she heard a voice speaking to her. The voice came from the movie. The voice gave her his name and told her that he wanted to get in contact with her. Because the voice insisted, she ended up accepting and a demonic spirit came in her. She felt something coming on her and immediately grasped her mother's hand. She bluntly stood up and said: "Mum! We have to go! We have to go!". They hastily left the room, her mother not really knowing what was happening. From that day on, this young girl was possessed by the spirit, to whom she would regularly talk. As they were about to pray for a "disease", it was actually for a demonic possession. How come neither the pastors, nor the parents saw that it was about that? Because of a lack of knowledge and discernment.

As you can see, ignorance can destroy individuals. That is the reason why the Bible tells us: *"My people are destroyed from lack of knowledge."* (Hosea 4:6). Understanding the spiritual world enables us to have a better perception of the society in which we live, and thus to have an enlightened and different look in relationship to some situations or some behaviors. Very few people realize that beyond some attitudes or some dramatic events hides demonic influence which main mission is to destroy. Consequently, to control the masses, the devil strives to find people he will be able to influence by making them accept his ideas, so that they can spread them in their turn.

It is essential for us to learn how to discern things, even if what used to be hidden and restricted to some insiders, increasingly starts going out in broad daylight. These last years, a large number of cartoons, books, films, series (for instance the series *Lucifer* on Netflix), have had the occult world as a topic, and have put forward witchcraft and magic. *Le Point* magazine released in October 2019 had an article whose title was quite evocative: "Witches are back". The whole was written in a very conciliatory tone. They have also released a special issue: "The witches - The story of a renaissance." *Le Journal du Dimanche* also published on November 3, 2019, an opinion column on the same subject, in which two hundred personalities called witches from all countries to unite. Among the signatories, women from the political, artistic and other spheres are to be found. One day, I was talking with a sales person from Fnac stores, who was working in the literature department. He told me that the best book sales in personal development were works about witches. He made me smile, because he told me in a naive tone: "I don't really understand the interest of people for these books." I did not answer him anything, even if I quite well understand what their interest can be. The aim is to make witchcraft and magic as attractive as possible, to initiate as many people as possible, so that they can open spiritual doors through that and in this way give access to demonic spiritual forces in their life. But fortunately, I observe that more and more people start realizing it, including non-believing people. Many of them do not hesitate by the way to denounce that on social networks and on their YouTube channel, to warn the biggest number of people. Many people do not care about that, either because they do not believe it, or because they do not see any danger. However, it calls to mind many others and their eyes little by little start to open on this reality.

2 - Learning to see how God sees

Paul, the apostle, wrote: *"Do not conform to the pattern of this world, but be transformed by the renewing of your mind. Then you will be able to test and approve what God's will is—his good, pleasing and perfect will."* (Romans 12:2). Even though some habits and beliefs have been present for a long time in society, sometimes we must have the courage to question what we have always believed in, to be sure that our perspective is really the right one, even if this must compel us to question our own identity. We do not always realize how easy it is to be influenced by the mentality of society, through media, television series, celebrities and social networks, and to let ourselves driven by the wave. In order to have the necessary hindsight, sometimes it is vital to see the bigger picture, to see things with another perspective, from Heaven to the Earth. The more you succeed in doing that, the more you free yourself from what kept you captive and away from the presence of God. Jesus said to his disciples that *although they were in this world, they were not from this world* (John 15:19). He wanted to teach them that their perspective has to be the one from the Kingdom of God, not from the world. It is a very difficult exercise, because the thought of the world is sometimes so deeply rooted in our hearts, that without deep renewing of our thought, we can be convinced that some principles of the world are in tune with God's, whereas it is not the case at all. The Holy Spirit and the reading of the Bible change the way we perceive the world surrounding us, so as to adjust our perspective onto God's. It is when we manage to see things not from our point of view, but from God's, that we start tasting what real freedom is, as it is presented to us in the Bible.

3 - Watching over our thoughts

Our life is led by our thoughts and everything that dominates our thoughts controls our life. If our thoughts are dominated by the thought of the world, we are in the grip of the god of this world, who is nobody else than the devil. The name attributed to him defines his nature, since the word devil means deceptive, slanderous. The god of this world strives to deceit human beings by infusing them with his thinking, which consists in taking them away from God's plan for their life. He uses guile by making them believe that God does not exist, that they do not need Him, that man is his own god and he is self-sufficient (Genesis 3:5). This approach leads most of the individuals to search for their personal pleasure, which explains individualism, selfishness, pride and wars, which plague society and have brought the modern world on the edge of the abyss. As for people who believe in God, he convinces them that life with God is austere, joyless, without any interest, and that true happiness is to be found elsewhere. This way, he tries to dissuade them by all kinds of seductions, and for those who are already well committed with God, he puts their resistance to the test, by attacking their faith through all kinds of hardships. The aim is to make them give up. The Bible repeatedly warns us against the stratagems of the god of this world, who has managed to blind the intelligence of human beings, by injecting them as a venom his thought in their heart. His coup d'état happened without weapons, without uproar. One single lie was enough for him to take the power of governing the Earth, that God had placed in the hands of Adam and Eve. Several centuries later, his strategy has not changed, it always remains the same. He extinguishes the light of the truth, to keep men and women in darkness, as we can see in this verse: *"And even if our gospel is veiled, it is veiled to those who are perishing. The god of this age has blinded the minds of unbelievers, so that they cannot see the light of the gospel that displays the glory of Christ, who is the image of God."* (2 Corinthians 4:3-4).

The question every one of us should ask to know what influences his thoughts and consequently his existence is: what dominates my life? Depending on the answer, you just have to go back to the spring to know who it is about. If your existence is led by God, the Holy Spirit should be your guide, for the Bible says: *"For those who are led by the Spirit of God are the children of God."* (Romans 8:14). By contrast, if your thoughts are dominated by the thinking of the world, your life is under the influence of the god of this world. The battlefield is mainly located on the level of thought, and the weapons used against you are all the information you receive over the time and that end up modeling your inner being. Once your inner being is formed, you interpret the world from what you have assimilated, and which makes up your thinking system henceforth. Your freedom depends on what you have believed in, and on the way you have classified all this information you have received. Questioning oneself is important, to consider if what you believed as being true really is and what you think is false as well.

The thought of the world leads us to focus our attention on the things below, and to be content with short-lived ones. It gives us a misshaped image of God and of ourselves, by giving us the illusion that we are independent beings and that we do not need Him to live. Our perspective comes down to what we live on the Earth, and as for the rest, we will see when the time comes. This is the dominating general thought today in our society, which pushes men to be content with their present life, but not to try to know more about it. Jesus has come to put on end to this approach, by bringing men and women to raise their eyes, to focus their attention on the things above, which have the particularity of being eternal. Throughout his ministry, He ceaselessly repeated that his Kingdom was not of this world (John 18:36), to stand out from the thought that dominates the world. If light is vital to the life of ecosystems, the spiritual beings that we are also need the light sent by God onto the Earth, that is to say Jesus Christ. This light is meant to enlighten all individuals, but the world unfortunately has not received it. Nevertheless, it remains accessible to all people yearning for it.

4 - Adopting a new thinking

The human being **is** spirit, he **has** a soul and he **lives** in a body. As soon as the person is born again, he immediately becomes a new creature, as it is written in the second letter to Corinthians: *"Therefore, if anyone is in Christ, the new creation has come: The old has gone, the new is here!"* (2 Corinthians 5:17). This transformation is made possible thanks to the instant regeneration of our spirit, by the Holy Spirit. The born-again man and woman experience at the beginning of their conversion a fierce battle between their spirit and their soul, because if their spirit is thoroughly recreated, their soul remains unchanged. That is why many people can have the impression of not really changing, because their habits, their thoughts, their convictions and their behaviors remain the same. Then a fight takes place between their new nature, that is to say their regenerated spirit, and their former nature, for the two have opposite wills. The body is also engaged in this struggle, notably through the flesh where lies the transgressive nature. The flesh relentlessly pushes human beings to act against the will of God. Paul the apostle explains very well the reason in his letter to Galatians: *"For the flesh desires what is contrary to the Spirit, and the Spirit what is contrary to the flesh. They are in conflict with each other, so that you are not to do whatever you want."* (Galatians 5:17). To end this battle, it is essential to strengthen our spirit, so that it is strong enough to dominate the soul, and that the two finally make but one. This way, we manage to gradually have the upper hand over our flesh.

- **Having the thinking of Christ**

The Bible teaches us that the thoughts of God are infinitely above Man's. In fact, God says in the Old Testament: *"As the heavens are higher than the earth, so are my ways higher than your ways and my thoughts than your thoughts."* (Isaiah 55:9). However, there is a very distinct difference between the human being who lives totally away from God, and the born-again man and woman, for the Holy Spirit being in them, they now have access to the thinking of God, as we can see in the following passage:

> *"For who knows a person's thoughts except their own spirit within them? In the same way no one knows the thoughts of God except the Spirit of God. What we have received is not the spirit of the world, but the Spirit who is from God, so that we may understand what God has freely given us."*
> (1 Corinthians 2:11-12)

Paul, the apostle ends this chapter 2 of the first book of Corinthians with the following verse: *"Who has known the mind of the Lord so as to instruct him? **But we have the mind of Christ**."* It can also be translated into: "We have the spirit or the intelligence of Christ." In other words, we are identical to Christ, so we must speak, think and act like Him. That is why the Bible tells us: *"As He is, so are we in this world"* (1 John 4:17). However, only the people who develop a real intimacy with his Spirit can discern his voice and truly adopt his thought. The distinction has to be made between religious people and people whose lives are directed by the Holy Spirit. Religious people obey God because they dread his punishment, whereas the sons and daughters of God obey Him because their thinking has become God's. Obeying is no longer considered an obligation for them, but rather a pleasure, because accomplishing the will of God is from now on logical and natural for them. The feeling of frustration that generally goes with the people who obey reluctantly, vanishes to give way to deep gratitude. Jesus himself would revel in making the will of his Father, to such an extent that He said one day to his disciples: *"My food,"* said Jesus, *"is to do the will of him who sent me and to finish his work."* (John 4:34). Those who adopt the thinking of God, also draw their contentment from the joy given to them by the making of his will. It is by making his will that they accomplish what they are on the Earth for.

• **Strengthening our spirit**

The more our spirit is strengthened, the more our life is led by the Holy Spirit, and the more we have the upper hand on our soul. Let us have a look together at the means by which a born-again person can strengthen his spirit:

The prayer in spirit: When someone is baptized of the Holy Spirit, he instantly receives the gift of speaking in tongues. Speaking in tongues is the supernatural language of our regenerated spirit. Consequently, the one who speaks with his intellect expresses the thinking of his soul, whereas who prays in tongues allows for the Holy Spirit to pray through his spirit. The Spirit expresses this way through his spirit mysteries neither understandable to the human being, nor to demonic spiritual entities, but the formulated language perfectly corresponds to the will of God for his life. Prayer in tongues enables to worship God, to intercede, to bring up to Him requests, to call to existence things that do not exist, remind Him of his promises for your life, and to search for his will. It is a powerful weapon, unfortunately neglected by believers, because they have not really grasped its use. The more someone speaks in tongues and the more he edifies himself up, that is to say he builds up his inner being: "*Anyone who speaks in a tongue edifies themselves, but the one who prophesies edifies the church.*" (1 Corinthians 14:4). The more his spirit is strengthened, and more the person is sensitive to the presence of the Holy Spirit, and able to discern his voice among the flood of thoughts overwhelming him every day.

The meditation of the Bible: Jesus said one day: "*Man shall not live on bread alone, but on every word that comes from the mouth of God.*" (Matthew 4:4). In the same way food is vital for human beings, a regular reading of the Bible also enables to feed the spirit. If diet is necessary for the physical body, spiritual food is essential for the spiritual body, because without that, the born-again Christian remains a purely carnal Christian, that is to say his life is ruled by his former nature, his emotions, his thoughts and his five senses.

Fraternal communion: With the increase of websites giving Christian teachings, conferences or many and various themes, it has become very easy to stay at home and to follow edifications from home. However, nothing will ever substitute neither the church nor fraternal communion, that is to say the fact of being united with brothers and sisters and to be together. The Church is in no case a mere building, but it is the assembly of one of several people who gather together, to be edified through teachings, to worship God, pray, exchange and encourage each other. The Bible says that: *"For where two or three gather in my name, there am I with them."* (Matthew 18:20). So, from the moment when two people get together and that Jesus Christ is the central subject, his presence is certain. In France, freedom of worship is guaranteed by the law of 1905, which enables in its first article the existence of churches, but it is not the case in all countries, particularly in China, where believers gather in secret places, notably in basements (underground churches).

The listening of the Word and testimonies: The Bible stipulates that: *"So faith comes from hearing, that is, hearing the Good News about Christ."* (Romans 10:17). When we hear about testimonies of conversion, or people having lived a liberation, a restoration, a miracle, a great gain or a professional promotion, this automatically strengthens our faith. The Word of God is not something static, it arouses faith, and faith surely pushes us to act. However, for this Word to be efficient and bring a deep transformation, it has to go from the stage of information to the stage of revelation, as seen earlier. The more someone lives experiences with God, the more his faith is strengthened because he realizes that the promises in the Bible are within reach, provided that he believes in them.

- **Your perspective determines your actions**

One day, Mary and Martha sent for Jesus, because their brother Lazarus was unwell. On learning the news, Jesus remained very quiet and said: *"This sickness will not end in death. No, it is for God's glory so that God's Son may be glorified through it."* (John 11:4). Jesus knew Lazarus would die, but his perspective was totally different from these two sisters', because He saw in the situation a way of manifesting the glory of God. And this is actually what happened, for four days later, Lazarus died, but Jesus raised him from the dead. This event had to happen for many people to believe in Him, and for Pharisians to decide to kill Him.

As most people would see a disease, Jesus saw a way to glorify his Father, because He had the right perspective. What about you? What do you see exactly? When you cope with a difficulty, do you see a way for God to step in your situation, and to be glorified? When you have financial hardships, do you see that as a way to see the favor of God? When somebody is ill, can you see the miracle? When some people around you bother you, do you manage to love them as God loves them?

You will certainly understand that what you believe determines the way you see and understand things. Always having the right look is important to see things as God sees them. It changes as the Word of God inscribes in you, as your relationship with God develops and as your faith strengthens. Someone who pleases the heart of God is someone who is constantly aware of his presence by his side, and for whom the reality of the Kingdom of God is superior to the Earth's. This person would then do every possible effort to have the same perspective as God's, so that the reality of the kingdom of God can take place on Earth: *"For the kingdom of God is not a matter of eating and drinking, but of righteousness, peace and joy in the Holy Spirit"* (Romans 14:17).

Chapter 3
Walking in the fullness of the Holy Spirit

> *"For the one whom God has*
> *sent speaks the words of God, for*
> *God gives the Spirit without limit."*
> (John 3:34)

Jesus needed the Holy Spirit to start his ministry on the Earth, that is the reason why He did nothing before having received Him. On the day of his baptism, the Holy Spirit came down on Jesus and drove Him to the desert, where He stayed forty days and forty nights. When He left it, the Bible tells us that He was *filled with the Holy Spirit's power* (Luke 4:14). It is from that day on that He could fully begin the work for which He had been sent. The Holy Spirit is the most unknown person of the Trinity, although He is the very first to clearly appear as soon as the second verse of the first book of Genesis:

> *In the beginning God created*
> *the heavens and the earth. Now*
> *the earth was formless and empty,*
> *darkness was over the surface of*
> *the deep, and **the Spirit of God was***

*hovering over the waters. And God
said, "Let there be light," and there
was light. (Genesis 1:1-3).*

The Hebrew word translated into God is *Elohim*, which is the plural of God: God<u>s</u>. It is important to point out this detail, because this subtlety does not appear in the English translation. We know today that behind the word *Elohim* hides the Trinity, that is to say three distinct entities, namely: God the Father, God the Son and God the Holy Spirit. In the same way the human being is spirit, soul and body, God also reveals Himself in three equal people. Throughout the Old Testament, the Holy Spirit appears on several occasions, but we do not have enough elements to really understand who He is, nor even what his exact role is. Only the coming of Jesus Christ enables to have a better understanding of who the Holy Spirit is and to realize how important He is. Many people reduce Him to a might or a power, but He is actually far more than that, He is someone with emotions, a will and desires. Only those who walk according to the Spirit, are truly pleasant to God the Father, because this is what He expects from his sons and his daughters, as shows us this verse: *"For those who are led by the Spirit of God are the children of God."* (Romans 8:14). It is vital to know Him intimately to let Him lead our life, because it is this way Jesus walked on the Earth, by being in perfect collaboration with the Holy Spirit.

1 - The person of the Holy Spirit, a peerless partner

Some time before leaving his disciples, Jesus introduced to them the Holy Spirit, by explaining to them that it is better for Him to go, so that the Holy Spirit can come (John 16:7).

He told them: *"And I will ask the Father, and he will give you another advocate to help you and be with you forever"* (John 14:16). The Greek word translated by advocate is *"parakletos"*, which means: advisor, advocate, intercessor, assistant, someone who provides help. The translation of the original Greek word is quite interesting, because it presents to us several sides of the Holy Spirit. Consequently, the Holy Spirit is the advisor, the intercessor, the advocate, the assistant, the comforter of born-again men and women. Some versions have chosen the use of the word *comforter* rather than *advocate*. His characteristics do not come to an end here, since the Holy Spirit is also described as being: *"the Spirit of **wisdom** and of **understanding**, the Spirit of **counsel** and of **might**, the Spirit of the **knowledge** and fear of the LORD"* (Isaiah 11:2). The Holy Spirit **in** us, is for our salvation and the Holy Spirit **on** us, enables the salvation of others, notably thanks to the overlay of power given to us by the baptism of the Holy Spirit. When someone is baptized with the Holy Spirit, he receives several spiritual gifts from the Holy Spirit. The gifts are not for him, but rather for the others, because they enable him to answer the needs to which the people surrounding him are confronted, and this way to manifest not only the power and greatness of God, but also his love. There are nine spiritual gifts, and they can be classified into three categories:

Inspiration gifts	Revelation gifts	Power gifts
Tongues	Word of Knowledge	Gift of Faith
Interpretation of tongues	Discerning of Spirits	Working of Miracles
Prophecy	Word of Wisdom	Gifts of Healings

I will not go into detail by explaining to what correspond these nine spiritual gifts, because I already largely deal with that in a former work entitled *The Revelation of God's Sons*. You can find in it all information if you wish to deepen this point. However, I would like to give you a concrete case, to show you the importance of spiritual gifts and their use. In this example, it is about the gift of prophecy.

I have a friend prophet whom God uses a lot, notably through the gift of prophecy. One day, as we were visiting friends in Columbus, Ohio, we made the acquaintance of a woman who could no longer have children. My friend told her the following thing: "God will give you another child. It will not be an adopted child, but a child you will have after a natural conception. I can see that in my spirit". When I heard these words, I stared at him, and my first reaction was to say to myself: "Brother, don't say that! Don't say such things!" You can quite well imagine that my faith was non-existent. Here, it was not about a global prophecy such as: "You will fulfill your destiny", or "You will influence your generation!", but it really was an accurate word. Knowing this friend well, I know that God has powerfully used him more than once, so I thought: "We'll see". One year later, this woman posted on Facebook a photo of her belly pregnant with the message: "The miraculous baby". Several weeks later, she gave birth to an adorable little girl. The prophetic word had enabled to activate faith in the life of this couple, to prepare them for the miracle that God was about to make in their life. As I am writing this book, I have learned that she was pregnant again.

When you become aware of who the Holy Spirit truly is, the look you have on Him and on yourself can but change, since you realize that his presence brings a lot of privileges to you. However, very few believers really realize that. That is the reason why there are many Christian people whose lives do not change, even though they are born-again. Despite many years of conversion, they are still confronted to the same situations and to the same hardships. The problem certainly does not come from God, but from the fact that they have not renewed their thoughts, by adjusting them onto their new nature.

Jesus asked his disciples not to leave Jerusalem until they received the baptism with the Holy Spirit (Acts 1:4). On the day when the Holy Spirit came down on them, the people in the place started speaking new languages, as a sign of the baptism with the Holy Spirit, and their life never was the same. The book of Acts tells us about the outstanding miracles that happened to the very first Christian people, giving thus birth to the Church. Some biblical commentators like naming the book of Acts "the Acts of the Holy Spirit", because when we study this book in detail, we realize that He is the main Author. Jesus has come to save mankind and reveal the Father. As for the Holy Spirit, He has come to reveal Jesus to the world. If Jesus could physically be in only one place at the same time, the Holy Spirit is omnipresent. King David experienced it, that is why he wrote in one of his psalms: "*Where can I go from your Spirit? Where can I flee from your presence?*" (Psalm 139:7).

2 - The role of the Holy Spirit

There are so many benefits to know the person of the Holy Spirit that Jesus Himself told his disciples: "*But very truly I tell you, **it is for your good that I am going away**. Unless I go away, **the Advocate** will not come to you; but if I go, I will send him to you.*" (John 16:7). Although the disciples were twenty-four hours a day with Jesus, He did not hesitate to tell them though: "***it is for your good that I am going away***". Can you imagine just a moment what their reaction was? Likewise,

Jesus said to his disciples: *"He will glorify me because it is from me that he will receive what he will make known to you."* (John 16:14). Without the person of the Holy Spirit, no one can have a deep revelation of Jesus Christ. No matter how some theologians spend hours studying the Holy Scriptures, the fact remains that as long as they are not born-again, as wide as their knowledge is, it only remains intellectual. **Knowledge brings information, but cannot transform you as long as it has not become a revelation.** I would like to show you some of the particularities of the Holy Spirit, to demonstrate how important his role is:

- **The Holy Spirit drives us to the truth:**
  *"But when he, **the Spirit of truth**, comes, he will guide you into all the truth. He will not speak on his own; he will speak only what he hears, and he will tell you what is yet to come."* (John 16:13)

- **The presence of the Holy Spirit is the token of eternal life:**
  *"And do not grieve the Holy Spirit of God, with whom **you were sealed** for the day of redemption."* (Ephesians 4:30)

- *"And you also were included in Christ when you heard the message of truth, the gospel of your sal-vation. When you believed, **you were marked in him with a seal**, the promised Holy Spirit, who is a deposit guaranteeing our inheritance until the redemption of those who are God's possession — to the praise of his glory."* (Ephesians 1:13-14)

- **The Holy Spirit gives out spiritual gifts:**
  "Now to each one the manifestation of the Spirit is given for the common good. To one there is given

through the Spirit a message of wisdom, to another a message of knowledge by means of the same Spirit, to another faith by the same Spirit, to another gifts of healing by that one Spirit, to another miraculous powers, to another prophecy, to another distinguishing between spirits, to another speaking in different kinds of tongues, and to still another the interpretation of tongues. ***All these are the work of one and the same Spirit, and he distributes them to each one, just as he determines.*** *"* (1 Corinthians 12:7-11)

- **The Holy Spirit calls:**
"While they were worshiping the Lord and fasting, the Holy Spirit said, **set apart for me Barnabas and Saul for the work to which I have called them.***"* (Acts 13:2)

- **The Holy Spirit speaks:**
"While Peter was still thinking about the vision, **the Spirit said to him***, "Simon, three men are looking for you. So get up and go downstairs. Do not hesitate to go with them, for I have sent them."* (Acts 10:19-20)

- **Only the Holy Spirit can convince someone to believe in God:**
"And when he comes, **he will convict the world of its sin, and of God's righteousness, and of the coming judgment***. The world's sin is that it refuses to believe in me. Righteousness is available because I go to the Father, and you will see me no more. Judgment will come because the ruler of this world has already been judged.* *"* (John 16:8-11)

To illustrate this last point, I would like to share with you a story I lived in 2017. During a stay in Africa, I went to visit incarcerated minors. I was with two friends who gave these youth literacy courses, as well as a pastor who worked in the prison. After having shared a short message to encourage them, my friend asked whether some of them were sick and were willing to receive the prayer. Several raised their hand and as he prayed for them, we attended several instant healings. After having finished, we started a song called *God is Able*. The teenagers who had been until then rather distracted, turned over their metal plate and started playing rhythmic music with their cutlery. After a few seconds, I could feel like electricity in the air. The more we sang and the more the atmosphere loaded with the presence of God. Suddenly, I looked on my left and one of the youths fell on his knees, crying. Then a second one, a third one and a fourth one. At the end, they were most likely more than twenty of them on their knees, crying because they were touched by the glory of God which was prevailing over this place. While I was observing them, the following verse came to my mind: "*When he comes, **he will convict the world of its sin, and of God's righteousness**, and of the coming judgment (...)*". We had done nothing special; we were merely witnessing the work of the Holy Spirit among these youths.

3 - The hand of God on the Earth

On the creation, the Holy Spirit was moving over the waters, when God said: "*Let there be light," and there was light.*" (Genesis 1:3). When the Holy Spirit heard the Word, He immediately produced light. The Holy Spirit is constantly in motion, waiting for the Word of God to act. Jesus is the Word of God; He declares the thought of the Father and the Holy Spirit materializes it. One day, Jesus cast a demon out of a dumb man. In the attending crowd, some people accused Him of having cast it out by Beelzebub, the head of demons (Luke 11:14-20). Jesus told them the following thing: *"But if I drive out demons **by the finger of God**, then the kingdom of God has come upon you."* (Luke 11:20). The Gospel of Matthew tells the same story, but the expression used by the author is very slightly different, as you can see: *"But if **it is by the Spirit of God** that I drive out demons, then the kingdom of God has come upon you"* (Matthew 12:28). When we compare the two verses, we can see a parallel between the Spirit of God and the finger of God. But this does not end here, I would like to draw your attention to the two following passages. On reading them, you will notice that it is exactly about the two same verses, except that the version is different:

- **Louis Segond version**
  *When I consider your heavens, **the work of your hands**, the moon and stars you have created: What is man, for you to remember him? And the son of man, for you to watch over him?* (Psalm 8:3-4)

- **New International version**
  *"When I consider your heavens, **the work of your fingers**, the moon and the stars, which you have set in place, what is mankind that you are mindful of them, human beings that you care for them?"* (Psalm 8:3-4)

The Louis Segond version has chosen the use of the word "hand", whereas the New International version uses the word "finger". This difference helps us picture in a better way one of the roles of the Holy Spirit, which consists in giving life to the Word of God. At the creation, Jesus, who is the Word, declared the thought of God, and the Holy Spirit shaped the moon and the stars and set them in place in the universe. The word had to be declared for the Holy Spirit to act, because the Holy Spirit acts in response to the Word of God. A glove is useless as long as it remains in some bottom drawer, because it is only when its owner puts it on that it fulfills its function. Likewise, a believer filled with the presence of the Holy Spirit may be compared to a glove, whose hand, being the Holy Spirit can act through it. A Christian filled with the Holy Spirit and submitted to the Holy Spirit consequently becomes the extension of the hand of God on the Earth. Every believer really must be filled with the presence of the Holy Spirit, for the will of God to be accomplished on Earth as it is in Heaven and this through him.

The first four verses of the book of John have quite another meaning, when we understand how every member of the Trinity works:

> *In the beginning was the Word, and the Word was with God, and the Word was God. He was with God in the beginning.* **Through him all things were made; without him nothing was made that has been made.** *In him was life, and that life was the light of all mankind.* (John 1:1-4)

The Holy Spirit was also actively involved in the creation of the human being, as we can see in the book of Job: "**The Spirit of God** *has made me; the breath of the Almighty gives me life.*" (Job 33:4). If we consider what we have just seen, we can imagine that when God said: "*Let us make mankind in our image, in our likeness*" (Genesis 1:26), the Holy Spirit heard these words and immediately implemented them by shaping Adam, the very first human being. Let us look in the book of Genesis how it happened: "*Then the LORD God **formed** a man from* *the dust of the ground and breathed into his nostrils **the breath of life**, and the man became a living being.*" (Genesis 2:7). We can see through these few passages that the Holy Spirit is far from the popular picture many people can have of Him, that is to say just a power or a force. The Holy Spirit is God on Earth, and the outstanding privilege He grants to born-again believers is that He lives in them (1 Corinthians 6:19).

4 - The importance of developing a communion with the Holy Spirit

Paul, the apostle ends his second letter to Corinthians with the following verse: "*May the grace of the Lord Jesus Christ, and the love of God, and **the fellowship of the Holy Spirit** be with you all.*" (2 Corinthians 13-14). The Greek word translated into communion is ***"koinonia"***, which means: fellowship, association, relationships, intimacy. You will agree with me on the fact that anyone who wishes to maintain good relationships with somebody else must show respect, attention, trust, integrity and sincerity. Without that, no real relationship can take place. It is the same for the Holy Spirit, if we wish to develop a good relationship with Him. The more someone spends time in prayer, the more he is filled with the presence of the Holy Spirit, and becomes this way a blessing for those surrounding him, because the Holy Spirit can fully act through him. The Holy Spirit can then bring a solution, a healing or a liberation, by communicating his life and his power through this person.

The role of the Holy Spirit is to lead us, to teach us, to advise us, to protect us and to transform us into the perfect stature of Christ, but for His job to be successful, we have to let Him have freedom to act in us as He wishes. As a consequence, every one of us must ensure Him an environment in which He will be comfortable to work, because the quality of the relationship we will develop with Him depends on that. From my personal experience, I would like to present to you seven points the Holy Spirit particularly appreciates in an individual and seven others that curb Him, or even grieve Him.

- **Seven points to develop a communion with the Holy Spirit**

  - **Obedience**: Making the will of God

  - **Love**: Towards God and towards the others

  - **Holiness**: Refusing sin

  - **Being aware of his presence:** Honoring Him by our behavior, our thoughts and our words

  - **Praying and worshiping in spirit**: The communion with the Holy Spirit enables to receive revelations and to open the doors of the supernatural

  - **Surrendering to Him completely**: The Holy Spirit can then make of us the extension of the arm of God on the Earth

  - **Walking by faith**: Without faith, it is impossible to please God (Hebrews 11:6)

- **Seven things that grieve the Holy Spirit**
  The Bible warns us against grieving the Holy Spirit (Ephesians 4:30)

- **Ignoring his presence**: Paying no attention to Him.

- **Resisting his voice**: Delaying to do what He asks us to do, or even disobey Him.

- **Anger, lack of forgiveness, critics**: This attitude grieves the Holy Spirit, which creates a separation between Him and us.

- **The lack of love**: Towards God and towards the others particularly grieves the Holy Spirit.

- **Living in sin**: By living in sin, our life is led by the flesh and not by the Spirit of God: *"So I say, walk by the Spirit, and you will not gratify the desires of the flesh. For the flesh desires what is contrary to the Spirit, and the Spirit what is contrary to the flesh. They are in conflict with each other, so that you are not to do whatever you want."* (Galatians 5:16-17)

- **The lack of fear of the Lord**: The fear of the Lord keeps us and protects us, because it pushes us to try to always have a right and humble heart before Him. But whoever has not got the fear of the Lord can easily fall into the traps of the enemy.

- **A wrong use of spiritual gifts**: Using spiritual gifts to put oneself forward, instead of looking for making Jesus Christ visible through us.

The more we study the Scriptures, the more the Holy Spirit reveals to us the mysteries hidden in them, not only to have knowledge, but also to learn to know the Father and the Son deeper. It is by discovering and understanding who They are that we grasp who we are in Them. In other words, without having a real closeness with the One who created them, and destined them to a goal, no man or woman will possibly know their own true self. Anyone who truly wishes to know Christ must endeavor to develop an intimacy with the person of the Holy Spirit, because He only can reveal to us who He really is. The Holy Spirit must become our friend and our confidant to establish a trust relationship with Him, for Him to be able to teach us, to lead us and to transform us in the perfect image of Christ. Someone according to the heart of God is someone who has managed to become intimate with the person of the Holy Spirit.

Chapter 4
Manifesting the hero

"No human being is born a hero, but he becomes one."

The Bible repeatedly shows us that, at some accurate moments in History, God called in men and women who had a particular destiny to accomplish a very specific mission. Whenever a special situation came up, God had already chosen and prepared beforehand the man or the woman who would take up the challenge. He has chosen Noah to build an ark, Abraham to be the father of a multitude of nations, Moses to free the people of Israel from slavery, Joshua to make them enter the country of Canaan, Gideon to fight the Midianites, David to contend with Goliath and to make the people of Israel a great nation, Nehemiah to rebuild the walls of the city of Jerusalem, Esther to dissuade the king from destroying the Israelites, Peter the apostle to build his Church, Paul the apostle to lay the foundations of Christianity and many others. Chapter 11 of the epistle to the Hebrews is called in most of the Bibles: "The heroes of faith", because it shows men and women who have shown faith, courage, obedience and persistence, sometimes even at the risk of their life.

We must definitely not forget the anonymous heroes, those men and women you will probably never hear about, but whose life is as important as others, because they have remained firm in their convictions and in making the will of God. "The heroes of faith" whose names have just been seen, would undoubtedly refuse the title of heroes if they were awarded it, because their humbleness steers them to consider themselves as normal people. They would surely tell us that they have had the privilege of having been chosen by God and to serve Him, and that they have done nothing special, except from willing to please Him. They would add that God has given them some abilities, and that they have done nothing else than to obey Him and to give up their life by living entirely for Him.

1 - A new race of believers

In the Old Testament, when God would choose a man or a woman to accomplish a particular mission, He would give them his Spirit. This way, we can see men like Moses, King David or Gideon who had the Holy Spirit **on** them, to accomplish what God expected from them. Gideon was a fearful man, who had no self-confidence, but on the day when the Spirit of the Lord came on him, his temperament totally changed and he was seized by divine boldness. Gideon was literally "clothed" with the Holy Spirit, as we can see in this verse: *"So the Spirit of the Lord **clothed** Gideon"* (Judges 6:34). David was also seized by the Holy Spirit (1 Samuel 16:13), and it is thanks to Him that he found the courage to confront a lion and a bear, and to fight the giant Goliath. Moses was also clothed with the Holy Spirit, so that God told him: *"See, I have made you like God to Pharaoh (...)"* (Exodus 7:1). When Moses needed the help of seventy elders to assist him in his task, God told him that *He will take some of the Spirit that is upon him, and He will put the Spirit upon them also* (Numbers 11:17).

In the Old Testament, the men and women who served God were considered as servants of God. In the New Testament, we observe the emergence of a new race of men and women, that the Bible calls sons and daughters of God. All the people who have accepted Jesus as their Savior and personal Lord, and whose spirit has been regenerated by the Holy Spirit, when He came to establish his dwelling **in** them, are called sons and daughters of God. The born-again men and women have privileged access to the Father, compared to their predecessors, as well as a greater dimension of intimacy with Him. In fact, their relationship is no longer based on a master-servant relationship, but on a child/Father relationship. That is the reason why God is no longer only their God, but He has also become their Father. This understanding tremendously changes the relationship we have with Him, as seen in chapter 2.

Jesus said to his disciples one day: "*I tell you the truth, of all who have ever lived, none is greater than John the Baptist. Yet even the least person in the Kingdom of Heaven is greater than he is!*" (Matthew 11:11). This passage is interesting, because it shows us a very clear difference between the men born under the Old Covenant (before the cross) and those born under the New Covenant (after the cross). Jesus considered John the Baptist as being the greatest among men, because he was filled with the Holy Spirit even from his mother's womb, and because he was the messenger sent by God to prepare hearts for repentance, in preparation for the coming of the Messiah. It is he who, when he saw the Holy Spirit coming down in the shape of a dove on Jesus, acknowledged He was the Lamb of God sent to save the men. Jesus said that the smallest in the Kingdom of Heaven was greater than John the Baptist, though.

Why did he say that? Because John the Baptist was not born again. The blood of Jesus had to be shed for the forgiveness of sins and the redemption of mankind, for reconciliation to take place, and for God to live in Man. The cross and the forgiveness of sins launch a new era: the sons and daughters of God.

In these particular times, God looks for people among his sons and his daughters who are ready to walk after his Son, to demonstrate his reality on the Earth, like Him. If many are called, few are chosen unfortunately (Matthew 22:14). In fact, although there are many believers, few of them are ready to commit themselves totally, by giving up everything to follow and manifest Christ. It is not a new thing by the way, because at the time of Prophet Ezekiel, God had already said: "*I **looked for** someone among them who would build up the wall and stand before me in the gap on behalf of the land so I would not have to destroy it, but I found no one.*" (Ezekiel 22:30)

Still today, God is looking for men and women who intercede day and night, so that He can spread his Spirit, and thus wake up his Church and nations. So, how will you answer his call? "Here I am!" or will you remain silent?

Manifesting the reality of the Father and the Son necessarily has a cost. You must be ready to accept criticism, mockery, even if it means ending up alone in some cases, to make Jesus visible through you. Some bravery is needed for this position, because it requires a separation between the world and God. It is in no case about secluding oneself in a desert island or stopping all relationship with the others, but it is about refusing to abide by the thinking of the world, because it is inevitably conflicting with God's. God looks for people who will not jeopardize their commitment with Him, genuine people who do not change their mind according to which way the wind is blowing, or which trend is fashionable, but who remain upright as to the values that are theirs, even when they are sometimes widely criticized within society. **The beacon of the lighthouse enables the boat to sail in darkness; likewise, the sons and daughters of God who are filled with the Holy Spirit shine in the midst of darkness, to lead towards their Creator his souls who go astray.**

Maybe you consider yourself unable, too weak, not qualified or courageous enough? Above all else, do not keep an eye on your own strengths, since God promises to give his Spirit, for you to be able to achieve what He expects from you. God likes using the weak, the people regarded with little respect, those voluntarily put aside by the system, to thwart the rules predefined by society. You just have to look at the different characters in the Bible, as well as the men and women who have gone down in the history of Christianity, the revivalists, the reformers and the pioneers, to realize that they were not always conventional people. Jesus Himself was not conventional, that is the reason why religious people did not accept Him, since they could not believe that He could be the Messiah. Paul, the apostle also made this observation, that is why he wrote to the believers of the city of Corinth:

> *But God chose the foolish things*
> *of the world to shame the wise; God*
> *chose the weak things of the world*
> *to shame the strong. God chose the*
> *lowly things of this world and the*
> *despised things — and the things*
> *that are not — to nullify the things*
> *that are.* (1 Corinthians 1:27-28)

2 - A new generation of heroes

For several years now, I have taken care of young adults as part of my local church. In June 2019, we decided to organize a weekend in Normandy, which topic was: "Heroes". Laurent, a pastor friend to whom I had asked to bring a message Friday evening on this subject, did not understand why I entitled that conference this way. According to him, Christians were not heroes in the sense that Jesus Christ accomplished everything on the cross, and that it is the Holy Spirit who gives us every day the ability to walk according to the will of God. I explained to him that I understood what he meant, but the level of temptation and of sin was such today, compared with about twenty years earlier, that I considered that a young adult who would manage to walk in the steps of Jesus Christ, without any compromise, was, according to me, a hero or a heroine. The Holy Spirit gives us the ability and the strength, it is true, but everybody is free to say "yes" or "no", when faced with temptation and compromise. When someone says "yes" to God, and lets Him act freely in him without limiting Him, he can then expect to make infinitely beyond everything he can ask or imagine.

During our retreat with the youth, we took the time for prayer and worshiping on Saturday evening, and three people asked the prayer because of spiritual oppression they would suffer. As we were praying, unclean spirits started to be seen, and the power of God came to liberate them. Did not Jesus say that He had come to set the captives free? Here is one of the mandates and one of the privileges He has left to those who choose to follow Him.

On a visit to a friend who was hospitalized in the emergency department, while we were talking, I suddenly heard a yell coming from the corridor. As I was surprised, I asked him what it was about, and he explained to me that an old lady had arrived in the evening and that she had shrieked all night long. How could an old woman have such a powerful voice? I suspected that it was in all likelihood one or several unclean spirits who were responsible for her state. I asked him if the nurses knew that it was certainly a demonic possession and he answered: "Of course not!". People have no idea how many people suffer similar problems as well, and because they do not know that Jesus can set them free, turn to doctors, psychologists, all sorts of psychotropics, unfortunately to no avail.

The title of "hero" used to be attributed to valiant warriors who had achieved a feat on the battlefield, by bravely confronting their enemies and preserving their freedom, as well as their people's. Back to the village, they were acclaimed by the population and lauded for their bravery, their fighting skills and their ability to have faced danger. If times have changed, the war for the conservation of freedom remains topical, though, except that this time it is about our freedom of thought. This nameless war is led in such a subtle way, that only those who have discernment enough can perceive it. The battlefield is nothing else but our thinking system, and one of his greatest enemies is conformism. To understand that, it has to be kept in mind that what dominates our thoughts controls our life. This way, somebody who wants to manipulate you no longer needs to use violence against you, he only has to make you believe things that will make you adopt a behavior that will turn out to be self-destructive over time. You will not be aware of that at all obviously, for you will be so convinced to achieve your own will.

Faced with this war, many have quit struggling and some have even never fought, thinking that they were free. But next to that, more and more people wake up and become aware of the situation now. They realize that their freedom of thought is jeopardized, because of the juggernaut of the one-track think-ing which tries to prevail by all means. You just have to look at political TV programs, reports, documentaries and TV news that relentlessly invite the same so-called "experts", for them to give their opinion on current events. The guests are carefully selected, to make sure that their words are always in accor-dance with this wish to standardize the thinking of the highest number. It is a sort of "evangelization" whose dispensed gospel is more used for dividing people than uniting them, stirring up fear and mistrust between individuals rather than peace, keeping people away from God. Of course, as soon as someone condemns this state of affairs, he is accused of conspiracism, to discredit the fact that he thinks differently.

Standing out from the others and becoming oneself has become a courageous act, because conformism dominates the modern world. All it takes is the will to no longer accept to follow the crowd, but to follow Jesus and Him only. Walking in the steps of Jesus is all but popular, especially in this day and age, because the gap is so big between the men and women who are erected as models in western culture, and the values advocated by Christ. The spirit of the world promises happi-ness to those who adopt his thinking, until they realize (quite often too late) that this was in fact just an illusion. As for Jesus, He has been honest from the very beginning, by explaining that walking by his side was a difficult and unpopular choice, but the benefit that would be obtained in eternity was priceless. We have to walk with our thoughts focused on Jesus at all times, to remind us that the only way to praise the Father is to do like Jesus: by perfectly accomplishing his will. In a world looking for heroes, they are not that far actually, because the hero is in you, in me, but we have to give ourselves up so that the real Hero, namely Christ, can fully manifest through us.

3 - Consecration

From a very early age, Paul the apostle was brought up in the tradition of his fathers. He was convinced to be on the right path, until the day when he came across Jesus Christ. He was so upset by this encounter that he devoted the rest of his life following and modeling the One he used to fight. This sudden turnaround is accounted for by the fact that the beliefs on which he had relied to build his identity no longer had any value whatsoever in his view. Indeed, the excellence of the revelation of Jesus Christ was by far superior to everything he had believed in before. Paul became a new man because he had discovered a new identity in Christ. During the time in his life when he was imprisoned, he wrote a letter to the believers of the city of Philippi, in which he explains to them the reasons why he had given up everything to follow Jesus Christ. Here is an extract:

the requirements of the law. I could consequently pride myself on having fulfilled all legal justice. Once, those prerogatives were as many subjects of pride in my eyes. But, because of Christ, I finally acknowledged their uselessness, I even learned to consider them as detrimental (if we become attached to them) and I rejected them. Indeed, I persist, still today, in denying them any worth. **I will even go further: everything seems a loss to me in comparison with the priceless privilege of having acknowledged in Jesus Christ my Lord. The most precious good, the one which, by far, surpasses all the others, is to know Him and to understand Him better and better. For the love of Christ, I have divested myself of everything, considering my assets as worthy of being thrown on the scrapheap when it is about reaching Christ. Only one thing matters to me: being recognized as being one of his own and being bound to him.** *I have given up looking for the approval of God on the basis of the accomplishment of a law. So, I no longer own any personal justice due to my own efforts.* **If I am fair in the eyes of God, it is because I have put my faith in Christ. Justice given by God comes from**

> *the faith and relies on it. But*
> *believing in Christ, trusting Him,*
> *is making his acquaintance more*
> *intimately. And this is precisely all*
> *my ambition: knowing him better*
> *and better; experiencing the power*
> *emanating from his resurrection*
> *and being as one with his suffer-*
> *ings, by dying with Him. Indeed, I*
> *yearn for being ceaselessly trans-*
> *formed by sharing his death[1]."*
> (Philippians 3:6-11)

On reading this passage, we have a better understanding of the reason why Paul gave up what seemed trivial to him, to focus on what he considered as honorable and true. Paul, the apostle perfectly embodied this new generation of sons and daughters of God whose life was utterly devoted to Christ and submitted to the Holy Spirit. In the manner of Paul, anyone who really wishes to please God the Father must also make the choice of giving up everything to walk in the steps of his beloved Son. This is possible as soon as he discovers the excellence of the grace found in Jesus Christ, as shows us this verse: *"For in Christ lives all the fullness of God in a human body."* (Colossians 2:9). This "giving up" translates into devoting to God one's time, gifts, talents, goals and passions, in a nutshell, one's life. However, what can seem like a loss on the human level is actually a benefit for anyone who understands that eternal life and true happiness are to be found in Christ. In other words, "losing" for Christ is getting satisfaction that is by far superior to everything you could have by "keeping" your life. In fact, **sometimes it is necessary to lose everything, to win everything.**

---

1. Original translation from the French Bible *"Parole de Vie"*.

Someone who wishes to have a heart according to God must consequently strive to do the three following things:

- **Consecrate one's time:** By giving your time to God, you bestow Him more room in your daily life, and those precious moments enable you to become more and more intimate with Him. You must know the following proverb: "Time is money". Indeed, time has a priceless value, since it cannot be made up. Based on this observation, it is important to have a good thinking about the way you use it, so as not to waste it uselessly, but to invest it in quality times, relationships and things that have a real value. The more you have quality time with God at your disposal, the more you end up being as one with Him, so much so that one day, He will call you his friend.

- **Consecrate one's heart:** By giving God the first place on the throne of your heart, you allow Him to lead your life, which ensures access to his peace and his joy and this whatever the circumstances. The result is that your life goals are totally reversed, because you no longer live exclusively for you, but for Him. The well-being it provides gives you enough love and strength to help the people around you.

- **Consecrate his will:** By choosing to submit to God, you become someone on whom He knows He can rely, because you enable Him to accomplish his will on Earth as well as in Heaven through you. Submission to God is in no case a loss of freedom, quite the contrary, for there is no greater mission for a human being than to work on the side of the One who renews his breath of life every day.

Conclusion

Let us endeavor to have a heart according to God and to make his will at any cost, and we will be the source of his joy. And who knows if, as King David, He will not call us his heroes one day as well? The time has come to wake up the hero or the heroine who deeply lies dormant inside you. It is an individual decision, whose cost is admittedly high, but whose benefits are unmatched. You will have understood through this work that it is in no case about the traditional hero or heroine, as we can know them in society. It is a matter of a new race of heroes having Jesus Christ as a model, men and women led by the Holy Spirit. To arm themselves, they have the Word of God as a sword, faith as a shield, and they draw their strength in the love that God has put in their heart for others. It is a battle which has to be done daily against ourselves first, by paying attention to our words, our behavior, our love, our faith and our purity. Each one of us must be an instrument whose main goal is to reveal Jesus. It is only by coming closer and closer to the image of Christ, that we will be able to revolutionize our society by making it better. The philosopher Blaise Pascal said one day: *"Man's greatness lies in his power of thought."* I take the liberty of using this quotation and slightly modifying it by saying: *"Man's greatness lies in his power of love."* Let us remember that at the twilight of our life, everyone will be judged depending on the love he will have manifested around him. When everything vanishes around us, only the love of God will qualify us to our final destination. I will conclude this book with these few verses from my composition:

> To love is one of the nicest
> verbs to conjugate.

> I love you, you love me, He loves you, He has loved us so much.

> True love is a spring wear where we have to draw from.

> It is endless, it fills the heart until overflowing.

> One drop of his love can change all mankind.

> It is freely accessible; it is called the everlasting God.

Table des matières